Testimonials . . .

Arlene Miller's books are among the very few grammar books worth reading. They are readable, applicable, and immediately useful. None of the many books I researched were very useful . . . until I found Arlene's books! —Hilary Moore: Actor-Director, Poet, @ Off the Page Readers Theater; and Teacher, Spanish@Work

To Comma or Not to Comma

"Arlene Miller's book *To Comma or Not to Comma* provides us with an easy-to-read, sometimes humorous, and very valuable handbook for those pesky grammatical and punctuation questions that pop up when writing. Although I'm generally pretty good at navigating the rules, there were many places in reading the book that I was surprised, or grateful, to understand the rule or the reasoning behind it—or I learned something completely new. Thank you, Arlene, for "comma-ing" to our rescue!" —Becky Parker Geist, Owner of Pro Audio Voices (audiobook production), President of Bay Area Independent Publishers Assn.

"An invaluable book for writers at any stage in their careers. It is a thorough and detailed guide about punctuation, done in a clear, concise and fun way. This book will help us write better books, and also blogs, articles, letter, emails and any written communication." —Brian Jud, author of 14 books (including *How to Make Real Money Selling Books*), and the Executive Director of the Association of Publishers for Special Sales

"I learned so much from *To Comma or Not to Comma*. There were rules I *thought* I knew, but Arlene showed me that I was doing it all wrong. I was completely messing up elliptical phrases and question marks with quote marks. Thanks to Arlene, I have a new tool to share with my writer community. A great resource." —Amy Collins, New Shelves Books

To Comma
or NOT
to Comma

Other books by Arlene Miller, The Grammar Diva

- *The Best Little Grammar Book Ever: 101 Ways to Impress With Your Writing and Speaking* (First Edition)—paperback and e-book

- *Correct Me If I'm Wrong: Getting Your Grammar, Punctuation, and Word Usage Right*—paperback and e-book

- *The Great Grammar Cheat Sheet: 50 Grammar, Punctuation, Writing, and Word Usage Tips You Can Use Now*—e-book

- *Beyond Worksheets: Creative Lessons for Teaching Grammar in Middle School and High School*—e-book

- *The Best Grammar Workbook Ever: Grammar, Punctuation, and Word Usage for Ages 10 Through 110*—paperback and e-book

- *Fifty Shades of Grammar: Scintillating and Saucy Sentences, Syntax, and Semantics from the Grammar Diva*—paperback and e-book

- *The Best Little Grammar Book Ever! Speak and Write with Confidence/ Avoid Common Mistakes* (Second Edition)—paperback and e-book

- *Best Little Grammar Workbook Ever! Use Alone or with Its Companion Book: The Best Little Grammar Book Ever*, Second Edition—paperback and e-book

- *Does Your Flamingo Flamenco? The Best Little Dictionary of Confused Words and Malapropisms*—paperback and e-book

- *The Best Little Grammar Collection Ever!*—paperback and e-book

- *I Wrote a Book: Now What? The Absolute Beginner's Guide to Self-Publishing*—e-book

Please post a review on your favorite website. Reviews are always appreciated.

To Comma
or NOT
to Comma

The Best Little Punctuation Book Ever!

Arlene Miller

THE GRAMMAR DIVA

bigwords101
Petaluma, California

To Comma or Not to Comma? The Best Little Punctuation Book Ever!

Cover art and design by Matt Hinrichs
Interior design and formatting by Marny K. Parkin

Publisher's Cataloging-in-Publication Data

Name: Miller, Arlene, author.
Title: To Comma or Not to Comma? The Best Little Punctuation Book Ever! 2018 | by Arlene Miller.
Description: Petaluma, CA : bigwords101, 2018 | Punctuation reference
Identifiers: LCCN 2018906968 | ISBN 978-0-9984165-6-4
Subjects: English language—Grammar. |English language—Usage. | English language—Grammar—Self-instruction.

Published by bigwords101, P.O. Box 4483, Petaluma, CA 94955 USA

Contact Ingram or the publisher for quantity discounts for your company, organization, or educational institution.

To Jake and Shelley,
My greatest loves and my inspirations

Contents

Introduction   1

Acknowledgments   3

Periods .   5

1. Declarative sentence   5

2. Command   5

3. Between two complete sentences   5

4. Indirect question   6

5. Abbreviations   6

6. Letters and numbers in a list or outline   8

7. Decimals   9

8. Elliptical expressions   9

9. Using periods with quotation marks   9

10. Initials   10

Question Marks ?   11

1. End of a sentence that is a direct question   11

2. End of a question that is shorter than a sentence
(elliptical question)   11

3. Embedded questions   11

4. Long direct question at the end of a sentence   12

5. Long direct question at the beginning of a sentence   12

6. Any sentence said in the tone of a question   12

7. Series of short questions at the end of a sentence   13

8. Using question marks with quotation marks   13

Periods and Question Marks Quizlet   **14**

Semicolons ;   **15**

1. Separate two complete sentences   15

2. Separate two sentences joined by a conjunction when there is a series in one or both parts of the sentence   16

3. Clarify a series where there are commas already in the items, or a compound sentence where there are already commas in each sentence   16

4. With *however* and *therefore*   17

5. Using semicolons with quotation marks   18

Colons :   **19**

1. Compound sentences—sometimes   19

2. Lists   19

3. Ratios   21

4. Salutation of a business letter or e-mail   21

5. Between the title and subtitle of a book   22

6. Introducing a quote   22

7. Time   22

8. Citations and bibliography entries   22

9. Biblical references   23

10. Capitalization after a colon   23

11. Using colons with quotation marks   24

Semicolons and Colons Quizlet   **25**

Parentheses ( )   **27**

1. Setting off additional information   27

2. Around numbers or letters in a list or outline   28

Brackets [ ]   **31**

1. Parentheses inside of parentheses   31

2. Insert an explanation or comment into quoted information 31

Parentheses and Brackets Quizlet   **33**

Hyphens -   **35**

1. Hyphenated words   35

2. Compound adjectives   36

3. Fractions   36

4. Numbers between 21 and 99 that are spelled out   37

5. Expressions of time   37

6. Separating a word at the end of a line   37

7. Spacing of hyphens   37

Dashes: En Dash –   **39**

1. Number ranges   39

2. Minus sign   39

3. Spacing around en dashes   40

Dashes: Em Dash —   **41**

1. Break in thought in a sentence   41

2. Do not overuse   42

3. Interruptions in dialog   42

4. Spacing   42

Hyphens and Dashes Quizlet   **43**

Italics (Versus "Quotation Marks")   **45**

1. Words, letters, numbers, and symbols used as themselves   45

2. Uncommon foreign terms   46

3. For emphasis   46

4. Thoughts versus dialogue   46

5. Titles: italics or quotation marks?   47

Quotation Marks " "   **49**

1. Direct quotations   49

2. Dialogue   49

3. Indirect quotations   50

4. Word or phrase from another person or source   50

5. Sarcasm or irony   50

6. Slang or intentional grammatical or spelling mistakes   51

7. Titles   51

8. Unusual use in a sentence   51

9. Definition in a sentence   52

10. Jargon   52

11. After *labeled* or *marked*   52

12. Around *yes* and *no*   53

13. With well-known sayings   53

14. Single quotation marks   53

15. Quotation marks with other punctuation   54

Italics and Quotation Marks Quizlet   **55**

Ellipses . . .   **57**

1. Omitted words   57

2. Trailing off at the end of a sentence   58

Apostrophes '   **59**

1. Possessives   59

2. Possessive pronouns   60

3. Plurals   61

4. Contractions   61

5. Apostrophes with other punctuation   62

Exclamation Points !   63

1. Exclamatory sentences   63

2. After interjections   63

3. Question said with emotion   64

4. Use with quotation marks   64

5. General rules for use   64

Ellipses, Apostrophes, and Exclamation Points Quizlet   65

And . . . Commas ,   67

1. Compound sentences   69

2. Series: The Oxford comma   70

3. Introductory elements   71

4. Setting off interrupting material   75

5. With *which* and *that*   77

6. In dialogue   78

7. Between two adjectives   78

8. With *etc.*   79

9. With *i.e.* and *e.g.*   80

10. Direct address   80

11. Addresses   80

12. Dates   81

13. With numbers   81

14. With *too*   82

15. With academic degrees   82

16. With *Jr., Sr.,* and other titles   82

17. Company names   83

18. Salutations and closings of letters   83

19. With *however* and *therefore*   83

20. Afterthoughts   84

21. Contrasting expressions   84

22. When *or* begins an explanation rather than a choice   85

23. To separate two of the same words in a sentence   85

24. To clarify when a word is left out   85

25. Unusual word order   86

26. Emphasis   86

27. Long question at the beginning of a sentence   86

28. Series of questions in a sentence   86

29. Clearing up confusion   87

30. Gray areas   87

31. When you do NOT use a comma   88

Comma Quizlet   90

Instead of This . . . Do This   93

Final Test   99

Appendix A:
Punctuation Marks You Probably
Don't Have on Your Keyboard   103

1. Interrobang ‽   103

2. Irony mark ⸮   103

3. Percontation/rhetorical question mark ⸮   104

4. The snark mark .~   104

5. Exclamation comma and question comma ‽   104

Appendix B:
Quizlet and Test Answers   105

Periods and question marks   105

Semicolons and colons   105

Parentheses and brackets   106

Hyphens and dashes   107

Italics and quotation marks   107

Ellipses, apostrophes, and exclamation points   108

Commas   109

Final test   110

Appendix C:
Glossary of Grammar Terms   **115**

Appendix D:
Your Quick Guide to Commas   **119**

Index   **129**

About the Author   **135**

Contact and Ordering Information   **137**

Introduction

Punctuation is often considered a part of grammar, but some purists separate them. Grammar concerns sentence structure and the placement of words. Punctuation consists of the little marks that all sentences contain to make them clear and readable.

Both proper grammar and punctuation serve to make writing clear and understandable to the reader. And it seems that punctuation causes even more confusion than grammatical issues. Take the "mighty comma," for example: *The Chicago Manual of Style* contains about 7 rules for the use of periods and about 60 rules for the use of commas!

Both periods and commas are included in this book, as well as our other punctuation friends: semicolons, colons, hyphens, dashes, apostrophes, question marks, exclamation points, parentheses, brackets, italics (close enough to a punctuation mark), quotation marks, and ellipses. We will even look at some punctuation marks we don't really use—and you may have never seen.

To Comma or Not to Comma is set up by punctuation mark, and several quizlets are included in addition to a final test. All examples are presented in boldface.

There are four appendixes:

A—Shows you several punctuation marks that might be new to you. They really aren't used, but would be useful.

B—Quizlet and Final Test answers

C—A glossary of grammar terms used in this book

D—A quick guide to commas. Just the rules and the examples from the comma section of the book.

A comprehensive index is also included.

Please don't hesitate to send me any comments or suggestions you might have for this book. As always, online reviews are greatly appreciated!

Acknowledgments

Where to begin . . .

First, thank you to Jake and Shelley, my children, who have given my life meaning for three decades now.

Thank you to Marny Parkin, my page designer; Matt Hinrichs, my cover designer; and Gil Namur, my website designer and maintainer. These three talented people—none of whom I have ever met in person—have been with me since my first books. They are all a pleasure to work with.

Thank you to all the members of Redwood Writers and BAIPA (Bay Area Independent Publishers Association)—both groups of which I am a member—for their continuing support and wisdom.

Thank you to all my friends who attend my book launches and talks; my social media friends; and those who read my blog posts.

And, of course, thank YOU . . . for reading this book and keeping up the good fight for good grammar and punctuation.

Arlene Miller, The Grammar Diva

Periods .

1. Declarative sentence

A declarative sentence is a regular old statement: not a question and not an exclamation. Ending a sentence is the simplest use of a punctuation mark. For example,

Paul Period held up a stop sign.

If you are saying or writing your sentence as an exclamation, use an exclamation point.

Paul Period dropped his big stop sign on a pedestrian's foot!

2. Command

A command is an order or request, otherwise known as an imperative sentence. It generally begins with a verb. It ends with a period unless it is said or written in an emotional way, in which case you could use an exclamation point.

Don't drop the stop sign, Paul.

Don't drop the stop sign on her foot, Paul!

3. Between two complete sentences

This is just a reminder that if you have two complete sentences, you usually use a period to separate them:

I am going to the movies. My sister is going with me.

You can also use a semicolon and a lowercase *m* in *my*. (I am going to the movies; my sister is going with me.)

You can add a conjunction (connecting word) and use a comma. (I am going to the movies, and my sister is coming with me.)

BUT YOU CANNOT USE JUST A COMMA TO CONNECT TWO COMPLETE SENTENCES. YOU WOULD BE CREATING A COMMA SPLICE, OR RUN-ON SENTENCE.

I am going to the movies, my sister is coming with me. (NO)

4. Indirect question

If a question is indirect, rather than direct, you use a period at the end of the sentence instead of a question mark.

Direct Question: Who is coming with us?

Indirect Question: He asked me who was coming with us.

5. Abbreviations

Periods are used in some abbreviations.

5.1 People's titles are followed by a period:

Mr. Jonas, Ms. Gonzalez, Mrs. Brown, Dr. Young, Phillip Yee, Esq., Martin Luther King, Jr.

Note: If an abbreviation that uses a period comes at the end of the sentence, only one period is used.

I was always in awe of Martin Luther King, Jr.

5.2 Abbreviations that are made up of all capital letters usually do not use periods:

IBM, FBI, YMCA, NHL, VIP (However, Washington D.C. does have periods.)

5.3 Some words in our language are merely "shortened" and should not have periods after them. They are not considered abbreviations.

typo, exam, memo, limo, logo, info, lab, rep, photo

5.4 The abbreviations *a.m.* and *p.m.* generally use periods (and lowercase letters unless you use the small caps: AM, PM)

5.5 The United States can be abbreviated to U.S. when you use it as an adjective, but it must be spelled out when you use it as a noun:

U.S. Navy

The population of the United States

5.6 The abbreviations of college degrees generally have periods after them.

B.A. M.A. Ph.D.

5.7 The abbreviation **OK** has no periods, but it is better to just spell it out (**okay**).

5.8 Measurements are often abbreviated, especially when they are used in tables. They should not be abbreviated when used in text. They generally do not have periods after them. One exception is *inch*. The abbreviation for *inch* (in.) has a period after it so that it is not confused with the word *in*.

ft = foot

yd = yard

m = meter

in. = inch

5.9 Some hints about using abbreviations:

Generally speaking, most abbreviations should be avoided in text; they are, however, fine to use in tables or graphs. In text, avoid using abbreviations for names of the months or days, measurements, etc. Titles, however (Mr., Dr., etc.), and college degrees (B.A.) are generally abbreviated in text as well.

There are so many abbreviations it is best to look up the correct punctuation of a specific abbreviation if you are unsure.

If an abbreviation or an acronym (an **acronym** is an abbreviated form of a name that uses all capital letters and is spoken as its own word, such as *OSHA* or *EPCOT*) might not be understood by your reader, it is customary to spell it out the first time you use it and to put the abbreviation or acronym in parentheses. After the first time you use it, you can use just the acronym or abbreviation.

Federal Bureau of Investigation (FBI)

6. Letters and numbers in a list or outline

Periods are usually used after the numbers in a numbered list, or numbers and letters in an outline:

Numbered List

1. Periods

2. Commas

3. Question Marks

4. Exclamation Points

Outline

1. Toy dog breeds

    a. chihuahua

    b. maltese

2. Terriers

    a. silky terrier

    b. West Highland terrier

7. Decimals

Periods are used as decimal points:

25.67

$5.75

3.14159265359

8. Elliptical expressions

An elliptical expression is a shortened version of what is meant to represent a complete sentence. They are followed by periods.

Careful. (meaning Be careful.)

Of course.

Good morning.

No doubt. (meaning I have no doubt.)

Do not confuse these elliptical expressions, which are usually fine to use, with sentence fragments—which are usually not fine to use. A sentence fragment is a group of words mistakenly used as a complete sentence:

Because it is raining.

Until you leave.

9. Using periods with quotation marks

There is a simple rule to follow when you need to use a period along with quotation marks (these rules are for American English—as opposed to British English):

Periods **always** go inside the quotation marks—no matter what.

Jane said, "I always remember that periods go inside quotation marks."

I love the old Beatles song "Let It Be Me."

10. Initials

People's initials are followed by a period.

E. B. White

A. Miller

However, no periods are used when letters are used to designate something other than initials.

Please compare Brand X with Brand Y.

Section A is completely full.

Question Marks ?

1. End of a sentence that is a direct question

The most simple and common use of a question mark is at the end of a sentence that is a direct question.

Is Quint asking us a question? (direct question)

I think Quint is asking if he should put a question mark at the end of that sentence. (Indirect question: no question mark at the end. Use a period or, if it is exclamatory, an exclamation point.)

2. End of a question that is shorter than a sentence (elliptical question)

Some questions may not be complete sentences, but you use a question mark after them too.

Is he coming with us? Why? When?

Had enough?

3. Embedded questions

If a short question is embedded within a sentence, set if off with commas, and use a question mark at the end of the sentence:

I can go with Quint, can't I, if I finish my homework?

Quint can ask a question, can't he?

4. Long direct question at the end of a sentence

When you have a long question that comes at the end of a sentence, the question begins with a capital letter and is preceded by a comma. The question mark goes at the end of the sentence.

The question is, Who is going to take Quint's place when he leaves?

I am still wondering, Who ate all the milk and apples?

5. Long direct question at the beginning of a sentence

When you have a long question at the beginning of a sentence, use either a question mark or a comma after the question, and put a period at the end of the sentence.

Who will take Quint's place after he leaves the company? is the question.

OR

Who will take Quint's place after he leaves the company, is the question.

Who will be left to lead the department? is my concern.

OR

Who will be left to lead the department, is my concern.

6. Any sentence said in the tone of a question

Sometimes we say a sentence that is actually a statement, not a question, as if it were a question, raising our voices higher at the end. Use a question mark after such a sentence:

Quint thinks he is going to graduation dressed like that?

You aren't going to work today?

7. Series of short questions at the end of a sentence

If you have a series of short questions at the end of a sentence, you can separate them with commas, as in a regular series, or you can use question marks.

If Quint isn't going to be here on Saturday, who is going to set up for the party, bake the birthday cake, and clean the house?

If Quint isn't going to be here on Saturday, who is going to set up for the party? bake the birthday cake? clean the house?
(Notice that the questions do not begin with capital letters.)

8. Using question marks with quotation marks

Question marks can go either inside or outside quotation marks, depending on the particular sentence:

Quinella asked, "Is Quint coming to the party?" In this sentence only the quoted part is a question. Therefore, the question mark goes inside the quotation marks. It belongs to the question only.

Did Quinella say, "I hope Quint is coming to the party"? In this sentence the quoted part of the sentence is not a question. However, the entire sentence is a question. Therefore, the question mark goes outside the quotation marks. It belongs to the whole sentence.

Did Quinella ask, "Is Quint coming to the party?" In this sentence both the quoted portion of the sentence AND the entire sentence are questions. We don't use two question marks. We put the question mark inside the quotation marks.

Periods and Question Marks Quizlet

Insert periods and question marks where necessary. See Appendix B for the answers.

1. Dr L Martin, PhD, is my psychology professor

2. She asked if I could go with her tonight

3. My cousin, Walter Hummel, Jr, used to work for the FBI

4. The doll measures 6 in in height

5. Did she say, "I can"t go with you this time"

6. Please meet me at my house at 7:45 pm

7. Here is my address: 54 Elm St, Albany, NY

8. Did he ask, "When will we be there"

9. He asked, "When will we be there"

10. After she left, I wondered, Does she know she has lettuce in her teeth

Semicolons ;

The semicolon might be one of the most feared of the punctuation marks, but it is really one of the most simple to use—and has very few rules.

1. Separate two complete sentences

The semicolon can be used to separate two complete sentences that are closely related. The other options are to use a period or to use a comma with a conjunction.

When we use a comma and a conjunction, we call the sentence "compound." The sentence is actually also compound when we use the semicolon instead of the comma and conjunction.

If the second sentence is a result of the first, you can also use a colon. However, the colon is not frequently used in this way.

Silly Semicolon has very few rules; this is one of them.

Silly Semicolon has very few rules. This is one of them. (Using a period is another option.)

Silly Semicolon has very few rules, and this is one of them. (Using a comma with a conjunction is another option.)

Silly Semicolon has very few rules: this is one of them. (Using a colon works, too, in this case because the second sentence follows something said in the first.)

Silly Semicolon has very few rules, this is one of them. (NOT an option; this is a run-on sentence because a comma alone cannot separate two complete sentences.)

2. Separate two sentences joined by a conjunction when there is a series in one or both parts of the sentence

If a compound sentence (two complete sentences joined by a comma and a conjunction like *and, but,* or *so*) happens to have a series in one or both parts of it, there will already be commas in the series. The sentence may be confusing unless a semicolon is added to separate the two parts of the compound sentence. This is best shown with an example.

This summer Silly Semicolon plans to visit France, Italy, and Spain, and her brother, Quint Question Mark, will be staying home. (not so clear)

This summer Silly Semicolon plans to visit France, Italy, and Spain; and her brother, Quint Question Mark, will be staying home. (clearer)

In the above sentence, you could omit the *and* after the semicolon if you wanted to.

Yes, there is another option. There is always the option of rewriting the sentence to avoid the problem.

Silly Semicolon plans to visit France, Italy, and Spain this summer, but her brother, Quint Question Mark, will be staying home.

3. Clarify a series where there are commas already in the items, or a compound sentence where there are already commas in each sentence

Read this sentence and see if you can tell how many people are going to the Town Picnic:

Hank Gomez, the police chief, a city councilor, Jack Freed, Abby Lee, the mayor, and the fire chief will all be at the Town Picnic on the Fourth of July.

The answer is Who Knows?

Try it again:

Hank Gomez, the police chief; a city councilor; Jack Freed; Abby Lee, the mayor; and the fire chief will all be at the Town Picnic on the Fourth of July.

The answer is five: (1) Hank Gomez, who is the police chief, (2) a city councilor, who is not named, (3) Jack Freed, whoever he is, (4) Abby Lee, who is the mayor, and (5) the fire chief.

The rule is that when you have a complicated series like this, you have two choices:

1. Use semicolons to separate the main items in the series, both the ones that have commas in them and even those that don't, if there are any.

2. Rewrite the sentence so that you don't have to deal with the problem. There are always multiple ways to rewrite a sentence. You could even make the series a vertical list in some cases.

Here is a compound sentence with commas that might make it confusing without the use of a semicolon:

My French professor was born in Lyon, France, and now lives in Tucson, Arizona; and Milan, Italy, is the home of his daughter, who also teaches languages in a university there.

Once again, you can rewrite the sentence to avoid the issue, which in this case would probably result in a better sentence anyway. You can also simply delete the conjunction (*and*) after the semicolon (use just the semicolon) to make the sentence read better.

4. With *however* and *therefore*

Often you will see *however* and *therefore* at the beginning of a sentence, where they are followed by a comma. Sometimes you will see *however* and *therefore* in the middle of a sentence, usually also followed by a comma. Sometimes there is a comma before them as well; other times there is a semicolon before them.

1. If I told you the answer to that test question, however, I would be helping you cheat.

2. I didn't know the answer to the question; however, I looked it up and found out.

What is the difference between example 1 and example 2? Why does the first sentence have commas surrounding *however,* whereas the second sentence has a semicolon before *however*?

The first sentence is one complete sentence with *however* used as an interrupter in the middle. Take out the *however.* You will see that you have one complete sentence. As an interrupting word, *however* is set off with commas.

Take out *however* in the second sentence. What do you have? You have two complete sentences. Since you cannot separate two complete sentences with just a comma, you need to use a semicolon between the two sentences. You can also make two complete sentences and use a period and a capital letter:

I didn't know the answer to the question. However, I looked it up and found out.

5. Using semicolons with quotation marks

You will not run across the issue of using a semicolon with quotation marks very often, but it does happen. For example, you could have some type of title that is set in quotation marks at the end of the first part of a compound sentence using a semicolon:

My uncle really loves the song "Moon River"; do any of you even remember that song?

The rule is very simple. Semicolons always go outside the quotation marks, no matter what.

Colons :

1. Compound sentences–sometimes

A compound sentence is two complete sentences that are somehow joined. We have already talked about using semicolons to join those sentences. And, of course, you can use a comma along with a conjunction like *and, but, or, so, nor, for,* or *yet.*

In some cases, you can use a colon to separate the two sentences, but only if the second sentence follows from the first or is a result of the first. Be careful; you can always use the semicolon or the comma with a conjunction, and you will be correct. But if you use the colon, it needs to be in the right circumstances. You do not usually capitalize the word after the colon. (Refer to Colon Rule 10.)

My mother loves to bake: she will bring a variety of homemade cookies to the party.

The special meeting is on Saturday: we will discuss the current financial situation.

You could also use a semicolon in the above examples.

2. Lists

2.1 Horizontal lists

A horizontal list looks like (and actually is) a sentence with a list at the end. A colon is used to introduce the list:

The recipe calls for these ingredients: sugar, flour, cocoa, butter, eggs, and milk.

However, if the sentence is written so that the list is finishing the sentence, you do not use a colon:

The recipe calls for sugar, flour, cocoa, butter, eggs, and milk.

In the first sentence, the words before the colon make a complete sentence: *The recipe calls for these ingredients.* However, in the second sentence, you would not put a colon before *sugar* because why cut the sentence off in the middle? *The recipe calls for* is not a sentence; the list of ingredients completes the sentence.

2.2 Vertical Lists

Vertical lists are treated the same as horizontal lists. Here are some examples of vertical lists:

Please bring the following items:
> **your textbook**
> **a notebook**
> **two or three pencils**
> **an eraser**

You use a colon in that list because the introduction is a complete sentence. But now look at this list:

Please bring
> **your textbook**
> **a notebook**
> **two or three pencils**
> **an eraser**

No colon is used in that list because the items in the list complete the sentence. Now look at this list:

Please bring
> **your textbook,**
> **a notebook,**
> **two or three pencils, and**
> **an eraser.**

Now look at this list:

You will need to do these chores while I am on vacation:
>   **Feed the dog and cats.**
>   **Water the plants and the lawn.**
>   **Take in the mail.**

All these vertical lists are correct.

Notice that there are periods after the items in the last list because they are complete sentences. Your list items should either all be complete sentences or no complete sentences. Make them consistent with each other. Of course, you can use bullets or numbers on your list items, but do not use numbers unless the order or the number of items is important.

3. Ratios

Colons are used to represent the word *to* in ratios, or proportions.

The odds of that movie winning the Oscar are 4:1. (four to one)

4. Salutation of a business letter or e-mail

If you are writing a business letter or e-mail, it is standard to use a colon after the name, rather than a comma. So if you are formal enough to use the person's last name, you might want to consider using a colon. Some people now use colons after the name on all memos, e-mails, and letters. That is fine, but be sure to use a colon if you are writing to someone you are not on a first-name basis with or someone at a higher level than you.

Hi Joe,

Dear Mr. Young:

Dear Mayor Kahn:

5. Between the title and subtitle of a book

While you don't generally see a colon between the title and subtitle of a book on its cover (although you could—it depends upon the design), if you are writing the title of a book in text, and you are including the subtitle, put a colon between the title and subtitle:

I am reading *To Comma or Not to Comma: The Best Little Punctuation Book Ever!*

6. Introducing a quote

You can use a colon to introduce a quotation. (In dialogue, however, commas are generally used before quotes.)

Mayor Jasper said yesterday, when speaking to the police department: "I am proud of the work you did last year. I look forward to another successful year."

The quote can be one sentence or more than one sentence. It doesn't matter.

7. Time

Of course, colons are used in expressions of time.

It is 3:35 p.m.

8. Citations and bibliography entries

Colons are used in **works cited** lists and bibliographies. The rules for citing resources could fill a book, so you will have to refer to the particular style guide you are following for those conventions. Here is just one example:

Miller, Arlene. *The Best Grammar Workbook Ever: Grammar, Punctuation, and Word Usage for Ages 10 Through 110.* Petaluma, CA: bigwords101, 2015.

9. Biblical references

A colon is used to separate chapter from verse in scripture references.

Romans 1:16

10. Capitalization after a colon

Here are some rules for capitalization directly after a colon.

10.1 Do **not** capitalize the words after a colon if they do not make a complete sentence.

My dog knows these commands: sit, stay, and come.

10.2 Do **not** capitalize the word after the colon if it begins a sentence that explains the previous sentence.

Several items will be discussed at the meeting: salary raises will be one of them.

10.3 **Do** capitalize the word after the colon if it begins a sentence that requires emphasis.

I will repeat the rule again: You are not to leave the house after 9 p.m.

10.4 **Do** capitalize the word after the colon if there are two or more sentences following the colon.

There are three rules to follow in this game: First, you must use all the letters. Second, you must complete the word in 30 seconds or less. Third, you must show your letters to your partner.

10.5 **Do** capitalize the word after the colon if it begins a quote that is a sentence (or more).

The judge said this in his decision: "We find you, the defendant, guilty of this crime."

10.6 **Do** capitalize the word after the colon if the word before the colon is a short introductory word.

Attention: You must turn right at the light.

11. Using colons with quotation marks

You will not run across the issue of using a colon with quotation marks very often. However, the situation might occur if you have some type of title that is set in quotation marks at the end of a sentence using a colon:

He talked at length about the article called "Ten Ways to Train Your Pet Cat": he explained he had trained over 1,000 cats.

The rule is very simple. Colons always go outside the quotation marks, no matter what.

Semicolons and Colons Quizlet

Insert semicolons or colons where necessary. You may have to change another mark to a colon or semicolon. Some sentences may be correct as they are. See Appendix B for the answers.

1. My favorite season is winter I really love to ski.

2. The title of the book is *Adopting a Dog Which Breed Is for You?*

3. Dear Department Chair

4. Major Jones said the following in his speech "I believe that the best is yet to come for the city."

5. I have visited Paris, France Rome, Italy and London, England.

6. We invited Mr. and Mrs. Greeley, our next door neighbors, Mr. Jagger, our realtor, and Mr. Thomas. (Assume that the Greeleys are the next door neighbors, but Mr. Jagger is not the realtor.)

7. Please bring a jacket, warm gloves, and extra socks on the hike.

8. Please bring these items with you

   - jacket

   - warm gloves

   - extra socks

9. I don't know what is wrong with my computer, however, the technician might know.

10. I have to wait for a phone call, then I can go with you.

Parentheses ( )

1. Setting off additional information

Parentheses are used to set off added information, usually of lesser importance to the sentence. You can put parentheses around single words, phrases, or complete sentences within a sentence. Sometimes a completely separate sentence can also be in parentheses.

Some people use dashes (—) to set things off in a sentence. Dashes are less formal and often are used more to emphasize something, whereas parentheses generally de-emphasize. Occasionally, commas are used to set something off that could be in parentheses, but you need to be careful there. A complete sentence cannot be set off with commas, but it can be set off with parentheses.

There is no need to add punctuation (like commas) before or after something in parentheses unless the sentence would have the comma(s) even without the information in parentheses.

Here are some examples of parentheses used with correct punctuation and capitalization. Note that even a complete sentence enclosed in parentheses within another sentence does not begin with a capital letter.

William Fumara (1925–2000) was my uncle and a very fine artist.

She misspelled the very last word in the spelling bee (*indiscretion*) and was eliminated.

The last place I look (as always) will be the place I find my keys!

Paul Parentheses wasn't happy with his grade in math (he received a B), so he decided to attend summer school to raise his grade to an A.

Paul Parentheses wasn't happy with his grade in math, so he decided to attend summer school to raise his grade to an A (he had received a B).

Paul Parentheses wasn't happy with his grade in math, so he decided to attend summer school to raise his grade to an A. (He had received a B.)

Although Paul Parentheses wasn't happy with his grade in math (he received a B), he decided to skip summer school and to party instead.

The sentences above are all correct. Here are some alternatives, both good and bad.

Paul Parentheses wasn't happy with his grade in math—he received a B—so he decided to attend summer school to raise his grade to an A. This sentence is fine.

Paul Parentheses wasn't happy with his grade in math, he received a B, so he decided to attend summer school to raise his grade to an A. This sentence is incorrect and a run-on (or comma splice). You cannot set off a complete sentence with commas. *He received a B* is a complete sentence.

2. Around numbers or letters in a list or outline

You will sometimes see parentheses used around letters or numbers in an outline or in a list. Sometimes only a closing parenthesis is used. Often when parentheses are used, there is no period after the number or letter.

Here are some examples. There is no right or wrong here. It is a matter of style.

Thursday's All-Day Meeting

I. Morning Session

    (a) Breakfast

    (b) Workshop

    (c) Practice Lab

I. Morning Session

    a) Breakfast

    b) Workshop

    c) Practice Lab

There are three things I need you to do after I leave: 1) Lock the door, 2) Clean up the kitchen, 3) Feed the cat.

There are three things I need you to do after I leave: (1) lock the door, (2) Clean up the kitchen, and (3) feed the cat.

Brackets [ ]

Brackets are really pretty easy to use. They have two main uses (other than math usage).

1. Parentheses inside of parentheses

If you should have the need to use parentheses inside other parentheses, use brackets inside the parentheses (not another set of parentheses). I don't think the need occurs very often, and I would recommend rewriting to avoid having to do it at all. It is possible that in very technical writing, you may have the need.

Here is an example of using brackets inside parentheses:

Please refer to the short article on page 75 of your textbook ("How to Use a Hammer," from *Tools Magazine* [June 16, 1975]).

Please refer to the short article on page 75 of your textbook, "How to Use a Hammer" (from the June 26, 1975, edition of *Tools Magazine*). Rewritten without needing brackets.

Please refer to the short article on page 75 of your textbook, "How to Use a Hammer," which is from the June 26, 1975, edition of *Tools Magazine*. Rewritten without brackets or parentheses.

2. Insert an explanation or comment into quoted information

If you need to insert something that is not part of the quote into quoted information, you use brackets, not parentheses. Sometimes when just part of a quote is used (in a newspaper article, for example), something that was said in the quote that the reader doesn't see needs to be explained. Other times, you just might want to insert a short comment into a quote.

Here are examples of both an explanation and a comment inserted into quoted material.

The mayor spoke to our club yesterday: "I applaud you all for supporting this great cause [funding for the new park], and I will be at the groundbreaking celebration next week."

The mayor spoke to our club yesterday: "I assure you I will help your fundraising efforts in any way I can [standing ovation] to get this public park built."

Parentheses and Brackets Quizlet

Insert parentheses or brackets where necessary. See Appendix B for the answers.

1. You can park all day for free the parking lot is on your left if you have a parking pass.

2. Please look at page 75 the figure of the dinosaur bottom left to see the complete skeleton.

3. The teacher was quoted as saying, "They the debate team will meet every afternoon to practice for the upcoming competition. We will win!"

4. Uncle Morris 1899–1990 was a famous artist in his native country.

5. If you are coming with us and that is up to you, you will need to take your own car.

Hyphens -

Hyphens are the short little lines you see inside words or at the end of a line of text. Do not confuse hyphens with dashes, which are longer and have different uses. There is a hyphen key on the number line (or number pad) of the keyboard.

1. Hyphenated words

Some words are hyphenated. Many of them are compound words (two separate words put together); others are not. Many times words are hyphenated after a prefix, for example, *ex-*. Here are some hyphenated words:

ex-husband

self-explanatory (Words with *self-* prefixes are generally hyphenated.)

anti-war (but antibiotic)

non-violent (but nonfiction)

semi-conscious

post-1950

e-book

Most compound words are actually not hyphenated:

eyewitness, salesperson, homeowner, workstation, checklist, trademark, airbag,

Some compound words are open, or written as two words:

school board, sales tax, money market

Many times a word begins as two separate words. When it becomes more common, it is hyphenated. When it becomes very common, it is often written solid, or as one word:

web site/web-site/website

e mail/e-mail/email

So how do you know whether or not to hyphenate a word? If you aren't sure, look it up. Often different sources will have different answers. One dictionary may say a word is hyphenated; another will say it isn't. What to do? Easy. Pick one way and stick to that way in a single piece of writing. Consistency is key.

2. Compound adjectives

A compound adjective is made up of two (or more) words that are placed before a noun to modify it. They are generally hyphenated when placed **before** the noun, but not hyphenated when they come **after** the noun. Here are some examples:

I like well-done steak. I like my steak well done.

She is a five-year-old girl. The girl is five years old.

This will be a hard-fought battle. The battle will be hard fought.

She is a self-made woman. That women is self-made. (*Self-* words are usually hyphenated regardless of where they are placed.)

I like the chocolate-frosted doughnuts best. I like the doughnuts that are chocolate frosted.

3. Fractions

Fractions that are spelled out are generally hyphenated. Mixed fractions (such as 2½) are often shown as figures since they are too long to spell out.

Two-thirds of the cake is gone.

I have about nine-tenths of my paper written.

The chicken will be done in two-and-a-half hours. (or 2½ hours)

4. Numbers between 21 and 99 that are spelled out

In technical types of writing, numbers lower than 10 are spelled out. Numbers 10 and above are usually expressed in numeral form. However, in writing in the humanities, we write out numbers up to 100. These numbers are hyphenated.

fifty-five, thirty-three, twenty-one, ninety-nine

5. Expressions of time

When expressing time in words rather than numerals, use hyphens.

five-thirty

seven-fifteen

6. Separating a word at the end of a line

Hyphens are used when there is no room for a complete word at the end of a line, and the word must be continued on the next line. With technology, this doesn't occur as much as it used to. Remember that you cannot split a one-syllable word or a proper noun at all. Also, remember to split words on their syllable breaks.

I am looking forward to summer vacation. Although I have a zil-lion things to get done, I will have some free time for fun.

7. Spacing of hyphens

There are no spaces before or after hyphens in any of their uses.

Dashes: En Dash –

The en dash is the short dash. It is longer than a hyphen, but shorter than the em dash, which is discussed in the next section.

To make an en dash on my Mac, I press *alt* and the hyphen at the same time. I hear it is the same on a PC, but then I hear that it isn't always. You can also use the Insert Symbol function and find the shorter of the dashes. Many people don't distinguish between the en and em dashes, and they simply type two hyphens in a row; sometimes your computer will combine them into a dash. Since en dashes are really not used very often, it is perfectly acceptable to use just one type of dash for "all your dash needs." However, do not use a hyphen as a dash. You need to use two hyphens for a dash.

Since the en dash and the em dash (or long dash) have different uses, I like to distinguish between them.

1. Number ranges

When you are indicating a range of numbers (or years), you use an en dash. You will often see the en dash, therefore, in an index.

John McDaniels (1919–1980) was a remarkable pianist.

sentences, compound, 25–28 (index entry)

2. Minus sign

In math, the minus sign is represented with an en dash.

75 – 50 = 25

3. Spacing around en dashes

The standard is still to put no spaces before or after an en dash. However, I do see spaces around number ranges and minus signs, so I say—whatever you want to do is fine as long as you are consistent within a piece of writing and sticking to what your editor or style guide says.

Dashes: Em Dash —

The em dash is the long dash. It is longer than an en dash, which was described in the preceding section.

To make an em dash on my Mac, I press SHIFT, *alt*, and the hyphen all at the same time. I hear it is the same on a PC, but then I hear that sometimes it isn't. You can also use the Insert Symbol function and find the longer of the dashes. Many people don't distinguish between the en and em dashes, and they simply type two hyphens in a row; sometimes your computer will combine them into a dash.

Since the en dash and the em dash (or long dash) have different uses, I like to distinguish between them.

1. Break in thought in a sentence

The em dash is commonly used to indicate an abrupt change in thought or idea in the middle of a sentence. Whatever is between the em dashes is, in effect, emphasized by that position in the sentence. Of course, the material set off by dashes can also be at the end of the sentence, in which case there is just the opening dash, as in the third sentence below.

My poodle—I cannot even believe she could do this—walked all the way downtown and home again!

Don't forget to buy candy—and you know the kinds I like—when you go to the grocery store.

You need to do this assignment by Friday—and I won't take "I forgot" as an excuse.

One thing to watch out for is that your dashes are in the right place in the sentence. Read the sentence without the words within the dashes. It should make sense. If it doesn't, your dashes are in the wrong place.

2. Do not overuse

Many people become "dash happy," tossing them this way and that. Dashes should be used sparingly in any type of formal writing.

Sometimes information can be enclosed in parentheses or commas instead of with dashes. If you are adding less important information, you will want to use parentheses instead of dashes.

I used the same textbook that you are using (but a different edition) in math class last year.

Many times you can also set off such information with commas, unless what you are setting off is a complete sentence.

I used the same textbook that you are using, but a different edition, in math class last year.

3. Interruptions in dialog

If you are writing dialog, the em dash is used to indicate that the speaker is being interrupted by someone else.

The worried mother said, "I see that you were not home by midnight as I told you—"

"Mom, I tried to call, but you didn't answer the phone," Marcy interrupted.

4. Spacing

As with the hyphen and en dash, there are no spaces around the em dash. Although you might sometimes see spaces around the en dash, generally you don't see them around the em dash.

Hyphens and Dashes Quizlet

Insert hyphens and em and en dashes where necessary. Some sentences may be correct as they are. See Appendix B for the answers.

1. The three year old girl was playing with a doll.

2. My dog he disappeared for over a week was found by my friend in the next town.

3. Please read the information on pages 6   8. (Place the correct mark between the numbers.)

4. The little boy is five years old.

5. Tom Bowers (1903   1969) lived in this house. (Place the correct mark between the numbers.)

6. I don't know perhaps you do what time the wedding begins.

7. I have seen a number of purple haired people in the parade.

8. That is my exboss over there.

9. "I see her right over there"
"Well, we can't get over there right now," she interrupted.

10. We are meeting our friends at six thirty.

Italics
(Versus "Quotation Marks")

Although italics (a slanted print style) are not technically punctuation, they are included here because quotation marks are often used when italics should be. Italics have uses that clarify writing and that should be mentioned here.

If you happen to be writing by hand (I think people still do that once in a while!), you cannot make italics. Don't even try. To indicate italics in handwriting, you simply underline.

1. Words, letters, numbers, and symbols used as themselves

When a word, letter, number, or symbol is used as itself, rather than as a grammatical part of the sentence, it is written in italics. Here are some examples:

I never can seem to spell the word *accommodate* correctly!

Which word comes first in the dictionary: *intrepid* or *interpret*?

I can see the large letter *E* on the eye chart.

You have mistakenly written the number *5* on the sign; it should be a *6*.

I don't like when my students use the *&* sign instead of writing *and* on their essays.

When an italicized word (or letter or number or symbol) is made plural, the *s* is not in italics.

There are too many *and*s in your sentence. (No apostrophe is needed before the *s*.)

2. Uncommon foreign terms

Uncommon foreign words and phrases are usually italicized, but the commonly used ones are not. Once a word or phrase becomes common in English speech and writing, it does not need to be in italics. Check a dictionary if you have questions.

The following words and phrases are common enough so that they do **not** need to be italicized:

a la carte, alma mater, bona fide, chutzpah, en route, et al., etc., non sequitur, per annum, per diem, magnum opus, rendezvous, savoir faire, status quo, summa cum laude, vice versa. (This is by no means a complete list of common foreign terms.)

3. For emphasis

Sometimes italics are used to emphasize a word or a phrase in writing. This is fine to do, but don't get carried away. Italics are best using sparingly for emphasis. It is better, however, to use italics for this purpose rather than boldface, quotation marks, or (oh, the horror!) all capital letters!

4. Thoughts versus dialogue

This use of italics occurs mostly in novels and memoirs. Quotation marks are generally used around dialogue (although occasionally these days you will run across an author who uses hyphens to indicate dialog). However, in cases where a character is thinking something rather than saying it out loud, italics are often used. You can say it is "internal dialogue." Notice that no quotation marks are used with the italics for internal dialogue.

"Julie, can you clear the table, please?" her mother asked as she thought to herself, *Why can't she ever remember without being told?*

5. Titles: italics or quotation marks?

One of the most common uses for italics is for titles of certain things. However, titles of other things are enclosed in quotation marks, and the two are often confused. Here are the standards for when to use italics and when to use quotation marks. The general rule is to use italics for complete things and quotation marks for parts of those things. Keep in mind that we are talking about using italics or quotation marks only when we are referring to these things in text. The actual title of the book is not in italics on the cover itself. A movie title is not in italics on the screen.

Italics are used for these: book titles; names of newspapers; names of magazines; movie titles; TV series or program titles; CD titles; pieces of art; titles of plays and operas; a poem long enough to fill a book; planes, boats, and spacecraft if they are given names other than their brand or model.

Quotation marks are used for these: short stories, short poems, chapter titles, names of acts or scenes in a play, song titles, names of a single episode of a TV series, newspaper articles, magazine articles.

Here are some examples:

***Of Mice and Men* is one of my favorite books.**

I was excited to see the *Mona Lisa* for the first time.

Please turn to Chapter 5, "The Anatomy of a Dog."

Did you see the launch of *Apollo 11*?

"Training Your Cat" is one of the articles in this month's *Your Pet Magazine*.

Quotation Marks " "

1. Direct quotations

Quotation marks are most commonly used to enclose direct quotations, which are the exact words said by someone.

Dr. Quinn Quote said, "I would really like some quail for dinner."

Quotes can, of course, be longer than one sentence long. Here is a multiple-sentence quote. Use quotes at the beginning of the quote and at the end, not at the beginning and end of every sentence.

Dr. Quinn Quote said, "I would really like some quail for dinner. And I love this particular restaurant because it is quite quiet. It is also quite quaint."

Sometimes a quote by the same person goes on for more than one paragraph. In that case, you put quotation marks at the beginning of each paragraph, but only at the end of the final paragraph spoken by that person. In this case, we are talking about a quote that is said all by the same person. This applies to dialogue as well, if the same person is speaking for more than one paragraph.

2. Dialogue

Dialogue is, of course, related to direct quotes. In dialogue, usually people are talking with one another. Quotation marks are used at the beginning and end of each person's speech. And remember, if you are writing dialogue, you need to begin a new paragraph every time the speaker changes.

"Quinn, this quail is undercooked," said Quentin.

"Mine is just perfect," Quinn replied.

"I am sending it back."

"Suit yourself. Mine is perfect."

As in quotations that do not appear as dialogue, if the same person is speaking for more than one paragraph in dialogue, you put quotation marks at the beginning of each paragraph, but only at the end of the final paragraph spoken by that person.

3. Indirect quotations

Quotations marks are *not* used in indirect quotations:

Sasha said that it supposed to rain this evening. (indirect)

Sasha said, "It is supposed to rain this evening." (direct)

4. Word or phrase from another person or source

Quotation marks are used around words or phrases that come directly from another person or source:

He claimed that he had a "surefire system" for beating the computer game.

The article said that if I use this beauty cream, I will have "ageless skin forever."

5. Sarcasm or irony

Words used in sarcasm or irony can be set in quotation marks.

The leader said that building up our weapons arsenal would lead to "everlasting peace."

He claims he is tall for his age. Yeah, he is so "tall" that he can wear kid's pants!

6. Slang or intentional grammatical or spelling mistakes

Slang words and expressions are put in quotation marks if they are not the usual way of speaking for that particular speaker.

My boss said his brain didn't have enough "bandwidth" to consider my idea.

She said she had gotten the book from the "liberry."

Note that you do not put quotation marks around misspelled words in dialogue. Misspelled words in dialogue are there because the speaker says it that way.

"Ah said it doesn't matter a'tall," she said in her Southern accent.

7. Titles

Some types of titles are in quotation marks, and others are in italics (see the section in Italics #5).

In a nutshell, large works are in italics, but parts of those things are in quotation marks.

Italics: book titles, magazine and newspaper titles, movie titles, CD titles, TV show titles, pieces of art.

Quotation marks: chapter titles, short story titles, newspaper and magazine article titles, song titles, TV episode titles.

If you are writing by hand or on a computer where you cannot make italics, you can underline instead. Some people choose to use quotation marks instead of italics in this case. Sometimes that is okay (on social media, for example, where your options are usually limited).

8. Unusual use in a sentence

Use quotation marks around a word or phrase that has an unusual or "abnormal" use or placement in a particular sentence.

This is a very "stick-to-your-ribs" casserole.

I didn't like her "I-am-better-than-you" attitude.

We need to "stick it to the competition" in order to win this one

9. Definition in a sentence

If you define a word in a sentence, put the definition in quotation marks.

Very few of the students knew that *defenestrate* means "to throw someone out of a window."

Note that *defenestrate* is in italics because it is being used as itself rather than as a word necessary to the sentence structure.

10. Jargon

Jargon is specific language that is familiar to a certain group of people; for example, there is legal jargon, technical jargon, medical jargon, etc. The first time you use a term that is considered jargon, put quotation marks around it. From then on, when you use it, no quotation marks are needed. If you are writing to an audience that understands the jargon, no quotations marks at all are needed.

We need to get the computer "booted up" before we can see what is stored in the "cloud."

To a group of technical people, this is everyday speech. But if you are talking to a group of people who have never owned a computer, well, that is a different story. You would need to put quotation marks around the words (and probably explain them too).

11. After *labeled* or *marked*

Quotation marks are used around words that follow *labeled* or *marked*.

I hope nothing is broken in that boxed marked "fragile."

That drawer is labeled "private," so perhaps we shouldn't look in it.

12. Around *yes* and *no*

You **do not** need to put quotation marks around *yes* and *no* unless they are part of a direct quote.

He always answers yes when I ask him a question.

When I asked him if he had gone out last night, he said, "Yes."

For each question, please just answer yes or no.

13. With well-known sayings

You **do not** need quotation marks around a well-known saying, idiom, or colloquial expression.

It's raining cats and dogs.

Those toys are a dime a dozen at the mall.

14. Single quotation marks'

There is only one use for single quotation marks. Do not use single quotation marks for any of the purposes described in 1 to 13 above (double quotes). The only use for single quotation marks is if you need to use quotation marks within something that is already in quotation marks. For example, if you have a direct quote from someone, and in that quote is a song title (song titles are in quotes), you will need to use single quotes around the song title. The other option is to rewrite, so you don't have something quoted within a quote.

She said, "My favorite holiday song is definitely 'Deck the Halls.'"

15. Quotation marks with other punctuation

Here are the rules for using quotation marks with other punctuation:

1. Periods and commas always go INSIDE quotation marks no matter what. (In American English. British English is different.)

2. Colons and semicolons always go OUTSIDE the quotation marks no matter what. (This doesn't occur very frequently.)

3. Question marks and exclamation points can be placed either inside or outside the quotation marks, depending on the sentence. If the question mark or exclamation point belongs just to the quoted material, it goes inside the quotation marks. It the question mark or exclamation point belongs to the whole sentence, it goes outside the quotation marks. If both the entire sentence and the quoted part are questions (or exclamations), use one question mark (or exclamation point) and put it inside the quotation marks. Here are some examples:

I think I heard little Quentin say, "Are we there yet?" (Only the quote is a question. Question mark goes inside the quotes.)

Did I hear little Quentin say, "I think we are there now"? (The quote isn't a question, but the entire sentence is. The question mark goes outside the quotes. And there is no period after *now*.)

Did I hear little Quentin say, "Are we there yet?" (Both the quoted part of the sentence and the entire sentence are questions, so use one question mark inside the quotation marks.)

Italics and Quotation Marks Quizlet

Put quotation marks and italics in the necessary places. You can use underlining for italics. Some sentences may be correct as they are. You may need to add a comma here or there. See Appendix B for the answers.

1. Please look up the word incoherent in the dictionary.

2. I would like my steak served a la carte.

3. He has a new boat, which he named Lucille.

4. I flew on a Boeing 757 to Miami.

5. You have used I to begin your sentences too many times.

6. Please turn to Chapter 2, The Order of Operations.

7. I was excited to see the movie Star Wars for the tenth time!

8. I always watch the television show From Now to Then, and my favorite episode is called Going to the Future.

9. Gone with the Wind is a great book.

10. I just sent for tickets to the play The Book of Mormon.

11. I hired her because of her I can do anything attitude.

12. There was an article in The New York Times called Children and Technology.

13. Judy said I think it is going to rain today.

14. Judy said that it will probably rain today.

15. The Mona Lisa is my favorite painting.

16. Please just answer yes or no!

17. It's raining cats and dogs this morning.

18. Yesterday is one of my favorite Beatles songs she said

19. I am running late she said, and I will probably miss the beginning of the movie.

20. The box was marked fragile, so I put it in the closet right away.

Ellipses . . .

I must confess. I have a real soft spot for semicolons. However, my least favorite punctuation mark is the ellipsis. Fortunately, I have had little reason to use it.

The ellipsis is used to indicate that something has been left out of a sentence, usually within a quote. It is also used to indicate a trailing off at the end of someone's sentence in dialogue.

1. Omitted words

The ellipsis is used to indicate that you have left out words, usually in a quotation. If you don't want or need to include the entire quote, you can use an ellipsis in place of the missing words.

The ellipsis itself is three periods with a space before and after each.

The speaker talked about his success: "I started my business when I was just in high school and began to make a profit . . . just a few years later. (There are some words missing here that the writer didn't feel were necessary for us to read. Perhaps they were "selling my widgets, and then I really busted loose in college.")

The speaker talked about his success: "I started my business when I was just in high school, . . . when I sold the business to my friend." (Notice there is a comma before the ellipsis in this example because there would have been a comma there if the words had been left in. Let's say the left out words here are "continued it in college, and decided to do something else after college.")

The speaker talked about his success: "I started my business when I was just in high school. . . . when I sold the business to my friend." (Notice there are four periods in this example. The first one is the period at the end of the sentence. Here, the words left out are the beginning of a new sentence. Let's say the words left out here are "I continued the business in college until I graduated,")

To sum it up, the ellipsis is three dots. However, if you are omitting words at the beginning of a sentence that comes after a complete sentence, the complete sentence still gets its ending period. If you are omitting words at the end of a sentence, the sentence still gets the ending period if what remains is a complete sentence. If the sentence is a question, use a question mark in either of these cases.

She said," How do you know that is true? . . . he said it is completely false." (Let's say the words left out are "I asked him many times and")

2. Trailing off at the end of a sentence

The most common use of the ellipsis is to indicate trailing off at the end of a sentence in dialogue. Refer to the chapter on em dashes to see that a dash is used when a speaker is interrupted in dialogue. The ellipsis is used when the speaker trails off.

Her mind was apparently on something else when she said, "I never realized . . ." (trailing off)

She said, "I never realized—" (interrupted)
"What do you mean, you never realized!" her friend shouted at her.

Apostrophes '

Apostrophes have only two primary uses, yet they are one of the most misused punctuation marks of all. You see apostrophes all the time where they should not be.

1. Possessives

When people think of apostrophes (if anyone actually thinks about them), they usually think: possessive. Yes, the most common use of the apostrophe is to show possession, or ownership.

To make most singular nouns possessive, you add an apostrophe and an *s*.

The baby's toy

The dog's bowl

My sister's dress

The woman's purse

To make plural nouns that end in *s* possessive, you add just an apostrophe. Some plurals don't end in *s* (*women, children*, and *men*, for example). To make those nouns possessive, add an apostrophe and *s*.

The babies' toys (more than one baby)

The dogs' bowls (more than one dog)

My sisters' dresses (more than one sister)

The women's purses (more than one woman)

To make singular nouns that end in *s* possessive, add an apostrophe and an *s*. You will often see just an apostrophe, but the standard is to add the *s* as well, even if it looks weird. You can generally go by how the word is pronounced. You would pronounce the singular possessive of *boss* with two syllables, right? And that is how you spell it:

my boss's desk (one boss)

the princess's slipper

Thomas's book

the bus's route

Here are the plural possessives of the above nouns:

my bosses' desks (more than one boss)

the princesses' slippers (more than one princess)

the Thomases' cars (using *Thomas* as a last name here and making it plural by adding **-es**)

the busses' routes (more than one bus)

Notice that the singulars that end in s and their plurals sound the same in the possessive, but are spelled differently: *boss's* and *bosses*.

There is an exception to the rule: If a singular word ends in an **-es** that is pronounced as **-ez**, there is no **s** after the apostrophe in the possessive: Socrates', Xerxes'. Also Jesus' has no added *s* after the apostrophe.

2. Possessive pronouns

The words we talked about in the section above are nouns (people, places, or things). Pronouns also have possessives, and there are NO apostrophes in possessive pronouns. Here are the possessive pronouns that end in *s:*

yours, hers, his, its, ours, theirs

Now you know which *its/it's* to use! The possessive one, in keeping with the rule, has no apostrophe: *its*.

3. Plurals

Generally speaking, plurals DO NOT HAVE APOSTROPHES (sorry for shouting). We see people putting apostrophes in regular old plural nouns all the time. I don't know why, and it is incorrect.

Social media post: **Look at my vacation photo's.** WRONG. It is just plain old *photos*.

Sign in the grocery store: **All apple's on sale.** WRONG. It is just plain old *apples*.

Very few plurals requite an apostrophe. When one is used, it is to make the word clearer.

I got all A's. With no apostrophe, you may think it says *As*.

You spelled this word with too many I's. With no apostrophe, you may think it says *Is*.

There are two u's in usual. With no apostrophe, you may think it says *us.*

You don't need an apostrophe in these numbers either:

I was born in the 1980s.

There are two 4s in my phone number.

4. Contractions

In addition to possessives, contractions contain apostrophes. A contraction is a shortened version of two words. The apostrophe is inserted where the missing letter(s) is.

it's—meaning "it is."

can't—meaning "cannot"

we've—meaning "we have"

she's—meaning "she is"

5. Apostrophes with other punctuation

Apostrophes are not like most other punctuation marks. They go with a particular word rather than with the entire sentence or part of the sentence. Therefore, an apostrophe is placed with its word, which would be inside any other punctuation.

I think these books are my sisters'.

3. Question said with emotion

You can use an exclamation point after a question that is said with emotion.

Wow! Did you see that huge dog!

Did you see that amazing sunset!

4. Use with quotation marks

If you are using an exclamation point with quotation marks, the exclamation point can go either inside or outside the quotation marks, depending on the situation.

If the entire sentence is an exclamation, rather than just the quoted part, the exclamation point goes outside the quotation marks.

I can't believe you said, "I don't know anything about that plan"!

If the part of the sentence in quotation marks is the exclamation, rather than the whole sentence, the exclamation point goes with the quoted part and is inside the quotation marks.

He shouted, "I can see the fireworks from here!"

5. General rules for use

Use exclamation points sparingly.

Do not use an exclamation point and a question mark together (!?).

Do not use more than one exclamation point in a row (unless you are writing something informal like a text or email to a friend).

Wow! Did you see that deer cross the road!? (Please don't.)

Wow!!!! What is that???? (Please don't.)

Exclamation Points !

Exclamation points are used to indicate words or sentences said with emotion, excitement, or alarm. They should always be used very sparingly. There is probably little use for them in formal, business writing—and maybe a little more use for them in fiction.

1. Exclamatory sentences

Use an exclamation point after a sentence said with emotion, but use this mark sparingly.

The house next door is on fire!

2. After interjections

An interjection is a word or short phrase said with emotion and sometimes followed by an exclamation point.

Wow!

Gee!

Darn!

Oh, my!

You might even have an interjection followed by an exclamatory sentence.

Yikes! The house next door is on fire!

Sometimes an interjection is part of a sentence and is followed by a comma.

Oh, that is a shame.

Ellipses, Apostrophes, and Exclamation Points Quizlet

Please correct the following sentences by adding or removing ellipses, apostrophes, and exclamation points. Some of the sentences may be correct as they are. See Appendix B for the answers.

1. I need to buy bread, milk, and apple's at the store.

2. "I think I forgot about," she said as her voice trailed off, leaving her sentence unfinished.

3. Yikes I left my wallet at the gym!!!

4. I found James' book in my locker.

5. Do you know if its supposed to rain today?

6. The childrens' clothes are getting wet out in the rain.

7. The dog left all its toys in the yard except the big green ball.

8. Do you know if these cookies are their's?

And . . . Commas ,

I was going to put the comma section in the "natural" scheme of things—maybe right before semicolons, but I decided to put them last. You might want to put a clip on this page, or a bookmark, or even fold the page over (oh, no, not a dog-eared page!)—or if you have an e-book, highlight or bookmark the page—because this is the section you will likely refer to most often.

Nothing confuses us more than commas. Some of us really don't like commas and don't know quite where to put them, so we don't. Others of us love commas and sprinkle them everywhere like salt or pepper. Many of us rely on the old "I will put a comma if there should be a pause there." That method actually does work—probably 75 percent of the time—but you cannot count on it.

The main purpose of punctuation is to make text clearer for the reader. Most punctuation marks are fairly cut and dried. A period tells you to stop; it is the end of a sentence. A semicolon also tells you to stop, but the sentence to come is closely related. Or maybe the semicolon is clearing up a messy sequence. The colon indicates that something is following, usually a list or series. A hyphen often tells you the rest of the word is on the next line, or that two words are being combined to make a new word. A dash is an emphatic change of course in a sentence. Parentheses indicate added, and less important, information. Brackets show missing information in a quote. Quotation marks surround the exact words someone says. Question marks indicate questions, and exclamation points show that something is said with emotion. Apostrophes indicate possessive nouns or contractions. What about commas?

Commas are intended to make writing easier and clearer to read, and most of the time they do just that. However, there are some instances where comma rules don't make anything clearer; it is simply standard to put a comma in.

In the world of commas, gray areas abound. I often have someone ask me if a comma goes in a certain place in a sentence; they are confused because one editor said yes and the other said no. Often, they are both right. Sometimes there is no answer, and it is up to the writer.

The examples in this section will probably be more valuable than the rules and explanations. And although there are a multitude of comma rules, here are the two main rules:

1. Don't use a comma unless you have a reason to use one. The legitimate reasons are either (1) "there is a rule" or (2) "the sentence is confusing without a comma here."

2. Use a comma anywhere where not using one would cause the reader confusion.

Let's just look at this example before we go into the standards for comma use:

Tommy and his mother ₁ went into the city ₂ on Saturday ₃ to go shopping ₄ and to visit his three sisters ₅ and five cousins.

The example above is a fairly long sentence. Notice there are no commas in it. You might be tempted to put one somewhere, but it doesn't need any. There is no place in that sentence that applies to any comma rule—and the sentence is perfectly clear to read without a comma—even though you might put a pause in there somewhere if you read it.

The **1** is between the subject (Tommy and his mother) and the verb (went). There is never a comma between subject and verb unless there is something set off in commas between them.

Tommy and his mother, along with his aunt, went . . .

The **2** is between two prepositional phrases. No reason to put a comma there. And you would have no reason to set off *on Saturday* with commas because you need that information in the sentence. However, there might be an occasion where you would set something off there.

Tommy and his mother went to the city, by the way, to go shopping . . .

The **3** is between two phrases, and there is no rule for a comma, even though you might put a little pause in.

The **4** separates two phrases: if there were three such phrases you would need a comma, but two things do not make a series.

Tommy and his mother went to the city on Saturday to go shopping, to see the new museum exhibit, and to visit . . .

The **5** once again is between two similar things, but two does not make a series. No comma before *and* when there are just two things.

Tommy and his mother went to the city on Saturday to go shopping and to visit his three sisters, five cousins, and two aunts.

And now, the rules . . .

1. Compound sentences

A compound sentence is two (or could be more) complete sentences joined by either a semicolon or a comma and a conjunction (*and, but, for, nor, or, so,* or *yet*). The compound sentence is one of the most common uses for a comma.

I am going to wash my car, and my roommate is going to mow the lawn.

I want the blue dress, Mazie wants the yellow dress, and Lenora wants the red dress. (Three complete sentences here. If you really, really, really don't want to use that comma before the *and,* you don't have to, but I would recommend that you do. See the next section.)

Are you going to the mall, or are you going to work?

I would go shopping with you, but I don't have much money to spend.

I will take out the trash, so you can sleep a little later.

If your compound sentence is really short, you can eliminate the comma.

I brush and I floss every day.

She knits and she sews beautifully.

Sometimes something that looks like a compound sentence isn't—and it doesn't get a comma. In the following example, read just the words after the *and*; you will find they don't make a complete sentence. Therefore, this is not a compound sentence:

She is going to her meeting at 10 in the morning and then is coming over here for lunch.

Now, take a look at the sentence below. It is not a compound sentence; it is a run-on sentence, and those are a no-no. The sentence is connected with the word *then*. However, *then*, is not a connecting word. It is not a conjunction like *and, but, for, nor, or, so,* or *yet*. You can correct this sentence easily and make it a compound sentence simply by adding *and* after the comma. You could also make it two sentences. I have seen sentences that begin with *then*.

She is going to her meeting at 10 in the morning, then she is coming over here for lunch. (Don't do.)

She is going to her meeting at 10 in the morning, and then she is coming over here for lunch. (correct)

2. Series: The Oxford comma

We use commas to separate the items in a series. A series can be made up of single words, phrases, or complete sentences.

I need to buy apples, oranges, bananas, and strawberries for the fruit salad. (series of words)

We are going to the mall, to the post office, to the pet store, and then to lunch. (series of phrases)

I am going to work, my husband is going golfing, and the kids are going to camp. (series of sentences)

So what about that final comma—the one before *and*? Do you need that one? That comma is famously called the Oxford Comma because it was first used by the Oxford University Press. Some people like to use it, and others don't. Some style guides recommend it, and others don't. Some teachers like it, and others don't. So if you need to follow a specific style guide or teacher, then please do. The Oxford comma is optional.

I have only two pieces of advice: (1) I use it and recommend that you do (unless you are following a certain style guide that says don't use it) because it often clears up the meaning of a sentence. (2) Using the Oxford, or series, comma is optional, but you should definitely be consistent in your use of it within a piece of writing. If you use it, use it all the time in that piece of writing. Here is an example of what can happen if you don't use the Oxford comma:

We invited the dogs, my sister and her friend.

3. Introductory elements

Many times a sentence begins with the subject:

My friends are coming over this evening to play Scrabble.

However, many times sentences begin with other words, phrases, or clauses. There is generally a comma (but not always) after these introductory elements.

3.1 Introductory expressions and transition words

In my opinion, it is too cold to go swimming. (introductory expression)

After all, the pool isn't heated. (introductory expression)

Yes, I think I will go to the pool. (introductory *yes* and *no*)

First, I think you should check the weather report. (introductory transition word)

Finally, make sure you check your essay for typos. (introductory transition word)

3.2 Introductory prepositional phrases

A prepositional phrase is a short group of words that begins with a preposition (*in, out, up, down, above, with, to, at,* etc.).You do not need to put a comma after a short introductory prepositional phrase, but you should use one after a longer prepositional phrase or two such phrases that are combined.

In France we will stay with friends. (*In France* is short. No comma really needed.)

In France last summer, we stayed with friends.

If the phrase is followed by a verb, you would not use a comma.

On top of the table sat a small dog. (The phrases *on top* and *of the table* are followed by the verb *sat.*)

3.3 Introductory participial and infinitive phrases

A *participle* is a verb form that usually ends in *-ing* or *-ed* that is not being used as a verb. It is being used as an adjective. Use a comma after an introductory participle or participial phrase. Make sure that when you begin a sentence with a participle or participial phrase, as in the following examples, you put the person doing the action described in that phrase right after the comma. In the last of the four examples, that wasn't done. That sentence is silly; we call that a misplaced modifier.

Hopping along the path, the rabbit stopped to munch a carrot.

Screaming, she ran from the house.

Throwing the ball, she shouted for me to catch it.

Reading a book by the window, the cat jumped into my lap.
(The comma is fine, but the cat didn't read a book by the window, so the sentence is incorrect: *While I was reading a book by the window, the cat jumped into my lap.*)

An infinitive is a verb phrase that begins with the word *to*. The verb in this case is now being used as a noun. Use a comma after an introductory infinitive phrase unless it is followed directly by a verb.

To be a doctor, you have to study for many years.

To go across the country, I had to change planes twice.

To be a doctor is my ambition. (No comma here. The phrase is followed by the verb *is.*)

If you see something that looks like a participial phrase, but is followed by a verb, don't use a comma after it. (It is not a participle; it is likely a *gerund*, but don't worry about that word.)

Going to the movies is one of my favorite things to do.

Playing the piano is a great hobby.

3.4 Multiple/combination introductory phrases

Sometimes you will have a combination of types of phrases at the beginning of the sentence, before the subject. Use a comma after such a combination.

Running into the house with his dog, Jeremy asked for a cookie.

To be a teacher in a college, you need an advanced degree.

During my vacation in France with my mother, I met some relatives for the first time.

3.5 Introductory clauses

A clause is a group of words that has a subject and a verb, but is not necessarily a complete sentence. The clauses we are talking about here, which might introduce a sentence, begin with such words as *until, since, because, after, before, although, whenever.* These clauses are followed by a comma.

Since I started college, I have been very busy!

Whenever I think of my cousin, I think of all the fun we used to have.

After I eat dinner, I will watch TV with you.

Because I work early tomorrow, I need to get to bed early.

Notice that all these sentences can be turned around, so that the introductory clause is at the end. When they are written that way, there is usually no comma. The reason why there is usually no comma is that the information in the clause (now at the end of the sentence) is necessary to the sentence. You might notice that you don't pause when you say the sentences this way.

I have been very busy since I started college.

I think of all the fun we used to have whenever I think of my cousin.

I will watch TV with you after I eat dinner.

I need to get to bed early because I work early tomorrow.

To make things more confusing, occasionally you will want to put a comma in a sentence with this type of clause at the end. In these cases, the information is not really necessary to the meaning of the sentence, and you might notice you pause when reading it.

I am not going to the party, although I did consider going.

4. Setting off interrupting material

Use a comma around elements that interrupt the flow of the sentence whether they are words, phrases, or clauses. **Usually.** If the element is required for the sentence to make sense, no commas should be used. Phrases and clauses that are necessary for the meaning of the sentence are called "restrictive." Commas are placed around "nonrestrictive" elements only. Sometimes it is hard to distinguish whether something is necessary or not, so just do your best.

Hint: The "pause" test usually works in these cases.

I know, by the way, all about your secret. (Added expression; not necessary, so use commas.)

It is true, of course, that I will be elected the new president of the club. (Some people may elect not to put commas around *of course*; I prefer the commas.)

I say, indeed, bring out the dessert!

The cake, chocolate with lemon icing, looks delicious.

Johann, my friend from school, was absent today.

Now things get a little more difficult; we need to distinguish between restrictive (necessary) and nonrestrictive (unnecessary) information.

Which of these is correct?

Harry's mother, Joan, is wearing the same dress as I am.

Harry's mother Joan is wearing the same dress as I am.

If you said the first one, you are correct. The second sentence treats Joan as necessary, or restrictive. Do you need to restrict Harry's mother to Joan? Does he have another mother? The second sentence implies that you are talking about his mother Joan, and not any other of his mothers. Since Harry has only one mother, put commas around *Joan.* Another way to look at this is to see if the two things are equal. *Joan* and *mother* are the same person. So you don't need both of them for the sentence to make sense.

This should become clear with the next example.

My brother, Josh, is staying with us for the weekend.

My brother Josh is staying with us for the weekend.

Which one is correct? In this case, it depends. The sentence with the commas is correct if I have only one brother. In that case, I don't need to identify the brother by name. The sentence without the commas implies that I have more than one brother. I then need the name of the brother I am talking about in the sentence. I am talking about my brother Josh, not my brother Bill or Ted. Therefore, I don't use commas; without saying which brother, the sentence is not as clear.

My neighbor across the street has a beautiful garden. (Which neighbor? *The one across the street.* Since that is necessary information, do not use commas.)

My neighbor, a teacher in town, has a beautiful garden. (Added information. Doesn't identify which neighbor.)

The cake with the white frosting is almost gone. (Identifies which cake is almost gone. No commas.)

The cake, which I frosted myself, is nearly gone. (This sentence implies that we already know which cake because we have used commas.)

The cake that I frosted myself is nearly gone. (This sentence implies that we are identifying which cake we are talking about because there are no commas.)

All the teachers who have been at the school for more than 20 years are being honored. (Identifies which teachers are being honored—only the ones who have been at the school for more than 20 years. No commas.)

All these teachers, who have been at the school for more than 20 years, are being honored. (Doesn't identify which teachers are being honored. Added information about the teachers who are being honored.)

Sometimes participial phrases interrupt a sentence. They are set off with commas:

My dog, running down the street, is going to get lost.

Sometimes there are just some descriptive words that interrupt the flow of a sentence:

My paper, due on Monday, might be late.

The sun, beautiful at sunset an hour ago, is gone from view now.

This coffee, much too strong for me, is perfect for my sister.

5. With *which* and *that*

Take a look at these two sentences:

This book, which is overdue at the library, took me a month to read. (nonrestrictive clause; added information)

The book that is on the table is overdue at the library. (restrictive clause; identifies which book)

Both of the above sentences have "interrupting" clauses. In the first sentence, *which is overdue at the library* is the clause. In the second sentence, *that is on the table* is the clause. (Although these clauses often interrupt a sentence, they do also appear at the end of sentences: The book on the table is the one *that is overdue at the library*.)

In that first sentence, the first word in the clause is *which*, and the clause is set off with commas.

In the second sentence, the first word of the clause is *that,* and the clause is not set off with commas.

Many people are confused about when to use *which* and when to use *that*. Most of the time, we use **which** with nonrestrictive (also called nonessential) clauses, where the clause is added information. We also set those clauses off with commas (and generally pause when we say them). We use **that** with restrictive clauses (essential information) and use no commas (and generally don't pause when we say those sentences.)

Which and *that* are usually reserved for things. What about people? **Who** is usually used with people in both restrictive and nonrestrictive clauses. You can use *that* or *which* with people, especially tribes or groups of people. I personally prefer to use *who* with people.

The boy who is sitting in the front row is my brother. (restrictive; identifies which boy)

The boy I was talking about, who is a straight A student, is going to Harvard next year. (added information)

The street names in my town are named after the Native American tribe that settled there so many years ago. (Here we used *that*—and notice that this clause appears at the end of the sentence, rather than in the middle.)

6. In dialogue

Commas are sometimes used in dialogue and direct quotations in places where you might think there would be a period: the end of a sentence. Here are some examples of using commas in dialogue and quotations.

"Have another piece of pie," he said.

"I would have another piece of pie," she said, "but I am trying to lose weight."

She asked, "Does this pie have much sugar in it?"

He replied, "It must. It tastes awfully good."

She thought before answering. " I don't really know the answer to that."

7. Between two adjectives

Sometimes we have two (or more) adjectives before a noun. Sometimes it is necessary to put a common between them; other times, there is no comma.

Here are two ways to help you figure out if you need a comma between the two adjectives:

1. You would pause if you said the words aloud.

2. You can put the word *and* between them and it makes sense.

Sometimes the first adjective is describing the second adjective rather than the noun. In that case, there is no comma. Here is an example. *Bright* is describing the kind of *blue*, not the dress.

She is wearing a bright blue dress.

Here are more examples.

Is that your new green bicycle? (*New and green bicycle* doesn't make sense. No comma here.)

That old, torn sofa is ready for the trash. (You would probably pause between *old* and *torn*; *old and torn* sofa makes sense, so you need a comma.)

Please take that dirty, smelly sneaker out to the garage. (*Dirty and smelly* sounds okay.)

I wish that pretty, redheaded girl would talk to me. (I might put a comma here; *pretty* could have another meaning: *fairly or sort of redheaded*)

Usually when one of the two adjectives is a color or a number, there is no comma.

8. With *etc.*

Use a comma before the *etc.* (etcetera—meaning *and the others*) at the end of the sentence. If *etc.* falls in the middle of the sentence, put commas both before and after it.

I like reading fiction, especially romance, chick lit, mysteries, etc.

Add the salt, sugar, flour, etc., before the wet ingredients.

9. With *i.e.* and *e.g.*

The initials *i.e.* mean "that is." The initials *e.g.* mean "for example." It is better to just write them out, but either way, they are set off with commas.

I love music from the Classical era, e.g., Mozart.

I love music from the Classical era, for example, Mozart.

The boy speaks only one language, i.e., English, his native language.

The boy speaks only one language, that is, English, his native language.

10. Direct address

When you are talking to someone using their name, regardless of where the name falls in the sentence, set the name off with commas. If there is a *yes* or a *no*, or possibly an interjection (word of emotion: *well, gee, oh*) at the beginning of the sentence before the name, that is followed by a comma as well. Check out these examples.

Jose, please bring the newspaper in.

Please, Jose, bring the newspaper in.

Please bring in the newspaper, Jose.

Yes, Jose, you can come over to play.

No, Jose, I am not going with you.

Well, Jose, it looks as if you got an A on that essay.

11. Addresses

On an envelope the only comma you need in an address is between the city and the state. There is no comma between the state and the zip code. However, you will need more commas if you are writing an address in text.

**Please send me the information at my new address, which is
124 Sunny Street, Boston, MA 02216.**

I live at 45 Elm Ave., Hunter, Idaho 67890.

I was born in San Francisco, California, in 1983.

We will be visiting my brother in Dallas, Texas, next month.

Notice the comma after the state in the last two examples above. It
may look a bit weird, but it is standard.

12. Dates

When you are writing the date on the top of a letter or somewhere else
where it isn't in the context of a sentence, use a comma between the
day and the year.

May 7, 2006

If you are writing the date without using the day, you do not need a
comma between the month and the year.

May 2006

If you are writing the date in text, you need to put a comma after the
year if you have included the day; if you have not included the day, no
commas are needed.

**My uncle has saved an article from the September 8, 1960, issue
of *Time* magazine.**

**My aunt has saved the photo of a dress from the March 2000
issue of *Vogue*.**

13. With numbers

Use a comma in numbers that contain four or more numerals.

5,000

7,000,000

If you happen to write a sentence that has two numbers in a row, you should probably rewrite the sentence. But if you don't, you need to separate the two numbers with a comma to avoid confusion.

Of the total of 575, 60 were children. (Obviously easy to rewrite in a number of ways.)

14. With *too*

When you use the word *too* to mean "also" in the middle of a sentence, you set it off with commas. However, if *too* comes at the end of the sentence, no comma is required before it.

I, too, would love to go to the concert.

Is Miranda coming too?

15. With academic degrees

Commas are used to set off academic degrees in text.

Colleen Comma, Ph.D., will be speaking about punctuation.

Sandy Sailor, M.A., is the guest at the meeting.

16. With *Jr., Sr.,* and other titles

Use a comma between the person's name and the title. However, if you are writing the name in the context of a sentence, you do not need a comma after the title unless something right after the title is set off in commas—or if the person prefers the title set off in commas.

Arnold Tyler, Sr. is my father.

Arnold Tyler, Sr., the director of the company, is my father.

17. Company names

Usually there is a comma before, *Inc.* or *Ltd.* in a company name. How-ever, you should punctuate the name as the company does, comma or not.

ABC Widgets, Inc. (But if they write it without the comma, you should too.)

18. Salutations and closings of letters

Put a comma after the salutation (greeting) of a friendly letter, e-mail, or memo. Business communication uses a colon, not a comma, in the salutation. The closing of a letter is followed by a comma.

Dear Mr. President:

Dear Joe,

Yours truly,

Sincerely,

19. With *however* and *therefore*

When *however* and *therefore* are used to begin a sentence, they are generally followed by a comma. When they end a sentence, they are preceded by a comma.

Therefore, I believe you should stick to the plan.

I am not sure the plan will work, however.

When *however* or *therefore* is used in the middle of a sentence, it is set off with commas. But be very careful; *however* and *therefore* are not connecting words, so if you have a complete sentence on both sides of *however* or *therefore* and no connecting word, you will need a semicolon or a period.

I know, however, that you will follow the rules. (Commas are fine here. How do you know? Take out *however,* and read the sentence. It still makes sense.)

I am not going, however, I know you will take notes for me. (Commas are not fine here. Take out the *however.* You have a run-on sentence.)

I am not going; however, I know that you will take notes for me. (Much better!)

I am not going. However, I know that you will take notes for me. (Also correct.)

Therefore works exactly the same way.

20. Afterthoughts

Usually, we use a comma before an afterthought at the end of a sentence. (If such a phrase comes in the middle of a sentence, use commas before and after it.) Sometimes the comma seems optional. Your choice.

He is traveling to both England and France, I believe.

Joe isn't coming to the party, by the way.

That dress is too short, in my opinion.

He isn't coming with us after all. (You could put a comma after *us.*)

I knew he was lying of course. (You could put a comma after lying.)

21. Contrasting expressions

Use a comma in contrasting expressions; they usually begin with *but, not,* or *rather than.*

I like pizza, but not with anchovies.

He is my cousin, not my brother.

Pepperoni pizza, rather than vegetarian pizza, is my favorite.

Here today, gone tomorrow.

22. When *or* begins an explanation rather than a choice

Sometimes we use *or* in a sentence to introduce an explanation of something we just said. In that case, it is followed by a comma.

The drum major, or the leader of the marching band, is my brother.

In the example, you are explaining that the drum major is the leader of the marching band. We are not presenting a choice of the *drum major* or the *leader.*

Would you like to be the drum major or the bass drummer? (In this sentence *or* is used in a choice. There are no commas.)

23. To separate two of the same words in a sentence

It rarely happens, and you should rewrite the sentence when it does, but occasionally you could have two of the same word in a row in a sentence. If you do, separate them with a comma to clear up confusion.

As she explained it, it is a new type of printer.

If that is what the situation is, is she going to be able to handle it?

24. To clarify when a word is left out

Sometimes a word is omitted from a sentence (usually *that*). Most of the time the sentence is still clear. Occasionally, a comma will help.

The reason for the delay is, his mother is coming all the way from New York. (The reason for the delay is that his mother . . .)

Usually, if you leave out *that,* the sentence is still perfectly clear without a comma.

I know she doesn't like us.

Here is another example of a comma used to clarify a sentence when words are omitted:

Girls between four and six should line up here; girls between seven and ten, over there. (Girls between seven and ten should line up over there.)

25. Unusual word order

If you choose to write a sentence that has an unusual word order, that is fine—but you might need a comma to clarify.

Why he is choosing that college, I will never know. (Usual order is *I will never know why he is choosing that college.*)

That you will be late for dinner, I completely understand.

26. Emphasis

Occasionally commas can be used to indicate emphasis, but I wouldn't overdo it.

I agree, completely, with your conclusion.

She, herself, is planning her entire wedding.

27. Long question at the beginning of a sentence

You can use either a question mark or a comma if you begin a sentence with a long question. Either of these is correct.

How is he going to get all that done in time, is my question.

How is he going to get all that done in time? is my question.

28. Series of questions in a sentence

You can use either question marks or commas if you have a series of questions in a sentence.

Who is going to bake the cake? decorate the room? greet the guests?

Who is going to bake the cake, decorate the room, greet the guests? (Using the commas implies that one person is going to do all these things.)

29. Clearing up confusion

A comma can be used in any sentence, when you cannot find any other rule, to clear up confusion.

After eating ants invaded our blanket.

After eating, ants invaded out blanket.

The dresses were pink with white polka dots and green with yellow polka dots.

The dresses were pink with white polka dots, and green with yellow polka dots.

30. Gray areas

One of the problems with knowing where to put commas is that sometimes you just have to decide for yourself. Sometimes the issue arises in a simple sentence, but more often it arises in a more complex and longer sentence.

Here is an example of a simple gray area:

Of course I will invite you. (Up to you whether to use a comma after *of course.*)

Here are some more complex gray areas. See the little question mark? You might or might not wish to put a comma there. I might be inclined to use the comma.

Dogs and cats, horses and zebras, lions and tigers—even a unicorn—they are all here in these short stories ₂ full of magic and mystery.

**"I want to be both a musician and the President when I grow up,"
said the little girl , without a second thought.**

**No one had cleaned the garage in many years , from the looks
of it.**

31. When you do NOT use a comma

So we have 30 standard uses for a comma. But there are times when
you don't use a comma.

31.1 Do not use a comma before a conjunction (*and, but, for, nor, or,
so, yet*) if the words that follow are not a complete sentence—unless it
is a series of course).

**He is going to the meeting and then might go out to dinner with
us.** (*then might go out to dinner with us* is not a complete sentence.)

**He is going to the meeting, and then he might go out to dinner
with us.** (*Then he might go out to dinner with us* is a complete
sentence. Use a comma.)

31.2 Do not use a comma before or after anything in parentheses
unless there would be a comma there even without the parentheses.
These sentences are both correct.

Turn to page 50 (the section on verbs) in your textbook.

**If you are coming with us (and I hope you are), please be here at
6 p.m.**

31.3 Do not use a comma between the subject and verb of a sentence
unless there are words, a phrase, or a clause set off in commas right
after the subject. These sentences are correct.

Jane and her brothers are meeting us at the theater.

Jane, along with her brothers, is meeting us at the theater.

Sean, Tim, and Brian are all brothers.

Bozo, my chihuahua, is really cute, isn't she?

31.4 Never put a comma between a verb and its object.

He threw the ball at his little sister.

He is baking a cake and some cookies.

He is baking, a cake and some cookies. (No.)

31.5 Do not put a comma between an adjective and its noun. These sentences are **not** correct.

It was a huge, textbook that we needed for math class.

There were seven, crayons in all.

This very old, dress belonged to my grandmother.

31.6 Do not put a comma between a noun or verb and a prepositional phrase that follows it. These sentences are **not** correct.

The kids are playing a game, in the living room.

The dog is lying down, on the sofa. (unless you are using this comma for emphasis)

31.7 Do not use a comma, even if there is a rule to use one, if it *causes* confusion. Here is a sentence in which there is a series that uses the Oxford comma.

Bob, my boss, and I went out to lunch.

How many people went out to lunch? Three? Or is Bob your boss? Taking the Oxford comma out (before the *and*) doesn't seem to help much, so the best thing to do is to rewrite the sentence. There are multiple ways to rewrite anything.

Bob, who is my boss, and I went out to lunch. (two people)

I went out to lunch with Bob and my boss. (three people)

Comma Quizlet

Insert or remove commas where necessary in these sentences. Some of the sentences may be correct as they are. See Appendix B for the answers.

1. It was a dark stormy night in New York City.

2. The book, that is lying on the table, is overdue at the library.

3. I love reading mysteries; however I don't really like thrillers.

4. In my opinion that dress is too fancy for a birthday party.

5. I don't like to cook and by the way I don't like to bake either.

6. After writing new ideas popped into my head.

7. In Rome do as the Romans do.

8. On the left side of the refrigerator sat the chocolate syrup I had been looking for.

9. She was looking for you so I hope she found you.

10. I went to the grocery store this morning and then came home and baked brownies.

11. I bought sugar, cocoa, baking powder, eggs and cinnamon.

12. Raymond J. Fox Sr. was my grandfather's name.

13. No Rosa I don't have any pizza left.

14. There are all kinds of books on the shelf e.g., mysteries, romance, science fiction and even some kid's books.

15. I got up at 6 a.m. and I didn't go to bed until after midnight.

16. Don't wait up for me because I will be home very late.

17. Since I am not going to the wedding I will mail a gift to the couple.

18. The letter was dated August 1999.

19. The cat was very tiny but very loud.

20. I am always right on time never late.

Instead of This . . . Do This

This section contains a summary of some of the most common punctuation slipups. Unless specified otherwise, the examples contain correct solutions.

1. Instead of putting an apostrophe in a plain old plural
Do this

Skip the apostrophe except in rare cases.

Did you see my photos?

How many a's are in the word accommodate?

I was born in the 1980s.

2. Instead of using a colon after a verb that introduces a series
Do this

Skip the comma if it comes after a verb.

Please buy bread, milk, sugar, and apples.

Please buy these items: break, milk, sugar, and apples.

3. Instead of using a comma after the greeting of a business letter, e-mail, or memo
Do this

Use a colon.

Dear Dr. Blumenthal:

Hi, Mary,

4. Instead of putting a comma between the subject and verb of a sentence

Do this

Don't use any punctuation between a subject and its verb.

James and his brothers, are going the game. (no)

James and his brothers are going to the game. (yes)

Angela, along with her sisters, is visiting. (The subject is just *Angela*; *along with her sisters* is added information. You can tell because we have used is, a singular verb, in the sentence. So the subject is also singular—just Angela.)

5. Instead of putting a comma between the verb and its object, or the verb and a phrase following it

Do this

Use no punctuation.

My cat and two dogs always have fun throwing, the ball. (Incorrect; take out the comma.)

I left my coat, in the theater. (Incorrect; take out the comma.)

6. Instead of putting a comma between the state and zip code

Do this

Put a comma between the city and state, but not the state and zip code.

My address is 10 Sunshine Way, Miami, FL 33655

7. Instead of using a comma to separate two complete sentences

Do this

Use a semicolon, add a conjunction, use a colon, or just make it into two sentences.

I am going into the kitchen; do you want anything?

I am going into the kitchen, so do you want anything.

I am going into the kitchen. Do you want something?

I am going into the kitchen: I will see if there are any bananas for you. (You can use a colon here if you want because the second sentence expands upon the first. But you don't have to.)

8. Instead of using commas to set off a complete sentence within a sentence

Do this

Use a dash or parentheses. You cannot set off a complete sentence with just commas.

I have been told, I don't know if it is true, that this tree is thousands of years old. (no)

I have been told—I don't know if it is true—that this tree is thousands of years old. (yes)

I have been told (I don't know if it is true) that this tree is thousands of years old. (yes)

I have been told that this tree is thousands of years old, although I don't know if it is true. (yes)

9. Instead of using an ellipsis to indicate an interruption of someone speaking in dialogue

Do this

Use a dash to indicate interruption (and an ellipsis to indicate trailing off)

Mom said, "Did you clean your room and take out the—"

"I already told you I was finished with everything," she shouted.

10. Instead of overusing dashes

Do this

Try using parentheses or rewriting the sentence.

The party—it will be held in the library—is tomorrow afternoon.
(Don't overuse the dash.)

The party (it will be held in the library) is tomorrow afternoon.
(yes)

The party, which will be held in the library, is tomorrow afternoon. (yes)

11. Instead of using a question mark and an exclamation point together to really make your point.

Do this

Choose one.

Can you believe he would say that to us!? (no)

Can you believe he would say that to us? (yes)

Can you believe he would say that us! (yes)

12. Instead of using quotation marks at the beginning and end of each paragraph in a multi-paragraph speech.

Do this

Use quotation marks only at the beginning of all the paragraphs, and then use quotations marks at the end of the final paragraph.

She touched on many topics during her talk. She said, "I know the company has had a huge decease in profits. We may have to wait another year before we see a turnaround.

"We are also aware that the construction that has been going on outside has been very disruptive.

"We will meet with the entire community next week to see if we can work on some plans to deal with the budget."

13. Instead of using single quotes to indicate a foreign word.

Do this

Use double quotations for unfamiliar foreign words, sarcasm, or words used in an unusual way in a sentence. Use single quotes only when you need quotation marks within other quotation marks.

She says she always does what will make her "the biggest winner of all."

14. Instead of using a semicolon to introduce any list

Do this

Use a colon to introduce most lists and to indicate something is to follow.

Use these three ingredients: eggs, sugar, and milk.

Use these three ingredients:

> **eggs**
>
> **sugar**
>
> **milk**

I give you my one word of advice: study.

Final Test

Correctly punctuate these sentences and phrases. Some of the sentences may be correct. See Appendix B for the answers.

1. I finished the project should I send it to you?

2. My sister along with her friends is coming to visit.

3. He said I heard the song Forget You

4. The new Star Wars didn't win the Oscar.

5. Bob was usually a quiet man however he screamed upon entering the room.

6. To whom it may concern

7. It is a cold rainy day.

8. This book which is written by William Golding is my favorite.

9. The book that is on top of the table is next on my reading list.

10. I decided not to cook dinner and went to the movies instead.

11. I packed these three items for my hike water a jacket and a knife.

12. I was born on August 10 1980 in Lincoln Nebraska.

13. The only four ingredients in this recipe are sugar vanilla eggs and flour.

14. I did not do very well on the test however so I failed the course.

15. I think you should pack these clothes for the trip jeans shoes black brown and white socks and three shirts.

16. Yes Elaine the party is at my house.

17. My address is 1487 Markham Place Boston Massachusetts 01987 please send my mail there not to my old address.

18. The word collaborate means to work together.

19. The self confident student was on the debate team.

20. Please read the information on pages 60   85. (Place the correct mark between the numbers.)

21. My six and a half year old cousin looks like my sister.

22. Jean Smith MD has just started to work here.

23. Although this food tastes terrible I will eat it anyway.

24. I failed the test because I didn't study.

25. I am running late she said, and I will probably miss the beginning of the movie

26. I love his can't fail attitude.

27. I can't believe since I didn't do anything wrong that I got fired.

28. Thomas' book is on the counter.

29. Did I hear you say, I am cleaning my room

30. That girl she was in my class last year is a cheerleader.

31. Whatever will be will be.

32. Why I can't speak French after all those years of classes I don't know.

33. "I don't know what I am going to do" she said, her voice trailing off.

34. Who is going to sit at the cash register when you are on vacation is my question.

35. I asked him if he could take care of the dog's when we are gone.

36. This summer I am visiting Idaho, Iowa, and Nebraska and my sister will be visiting cousins in Boston.

37. Charles Crumb (1874 1927) is buried here. (Put punctuation between the two numbers.)

38. Did you read the book Training Cats 101 Ways to Teach Your Cat Tricks

39. Hey Watch out for the oncoming train

40. I got all As on my report card the five year old student said.

Appendix A: Punctuation Marks You Probably Don't Have on Your Keyboard

While you might have to worry about the correct placement of a comma or semicolon, you probably won't have to worry about these punctuation marks that are either no longer used or have never been widely used, handy as they might be. You won't even find them on your keyboard.

1. Interrobang ‽

You don't want to use a question mark and an exclamation point together, as we already talked about earlier. However, you must admit that sometimes it would come in handy. Well, there is a mark that is a combination of the two: the interrobang. The interrobang is the most common of the uncommon punctuation marks and is actually in some limited use lately. However, I have never seen one. It might even be on some keyboards. Not mine.

What do you *think* I'm doing‽

2. Irony mark ⸮

The irony mark precedes a sentence to warn the reader that irony is coming. Writers have been talking about using irony symbols since the 1600s, but the first ones were printed in the 1800s.

⸮I heard that the scuba diver drowned in his bathtub.

3. Percontation/rhetorical question mark ⸮

This backward question mark was used until the early 1600s. It was proposed in the late 1500s as the ending to a rhetorical question.

Do you think I am made of money⸮

4. The snark mark .~

The snark mark is for sarcastic and "snarky" comments.

After how you bragged about your dancing skill, I thought you would be better than this.~

5. Exclamation comma and question comma ⸮

A Canadian patent was filed for these two marks in 1992, but it has lapsed, so feel free to use these marks if you can figure out how. How are they used? I guess if you want to be excited or ask a question before the end of a sentence.

I know she had yellow eyes; pink hair, and green lipstick!

Appendix B:
Quizlet and Test Answers

Periods and question marks

1. Dr. L. Martin, Ph.D., is my psychology professor.

2. She asked if I could go with her tonight.

3. My cousin, Walter Hummel, Jr., used to work for the FBI.

4. The doll measures 6 in. in height.

5. Did she say, "I can't go with you this time"?

6. Please meet me at my house at 7:45 p.m.

7. Here is my address: 54 Elm St., Albany, NY.

8. Did he ask, "When will we be there?"

9. He asked, "When will we be there?"

10. After she left, I wondered, Does she know she has lettuce in her teeth?

Semicolons and colons

1. My favorite season is winter; I really love to ski. *(You could use a colon instead of the semicolon here.)*

2. The title of the book is *Adopting a Dog: Which Breed Is for You?*

3. Dear Department Chair:

4. Major Jones said the following in his speech: "I believe that the best is yet to come for the city."

5. I have visited Paris, France; Rome, Italy; and London, England.

6. We invited Mr. and Mrs. Greeley, our next door neighbors; Mr. Jagger, our realtor; and Mr. Thomas. *(Assume that the Greeleys are the next door neighbors, but Mr. Jagger is not the realtor.)*

7. Please bring a jacket, warm gloves, and extra socks on the hike. *(correct as is)*

8. Please bring these items with you:

- jacket

- warm gloves

- extra socks

9. I don't know what is wrong with my computer; however, the technician might know.

10. I have to wait for a phone call; then I can go with you.

Parentheses and brackets

1. You can park all day for free (the parking lot is on your left) if you have a parking pass.

2. Please look at page 75 (the figure of the dinosaur [bottom left]) to see the complete skeleton. (*You could skip the brackets and just use a comma before* bottom.)

3. The teacher was quoted as saying, "They [the debate team] will meet every afternoon to discuss to upcoming competition. We will win!"

4. Uncle Morris (1899–1990) was a famous artist in his native country.

5. If you are coming with us (and that is up to you), you will need to take your own car.

Hyphens and dashes

1. The three-year-old girl was playing with a doll. *(hyphens)*

2. My dog—he disappeared for over a week—was found by my friend in the next town. *(em dashes)*

3. Please read the information on pages 6–8. *(en dash)*.

4. The little boy is five years old. *(correct as is)*

5. Tom Bowers (1903–1969) lived in this house. *(en dash)*.

6. I don't know—perhaps you do—what time the wedding begins. *(em dashes)*

7. I have seen a number of purple-haired people in the parade. *(hyphen)*

8. That is my ex-boss over there. *(hyphen)*

9. "I see her right over there—"
"Well, we can't get over there right now," she interrupted. *(em dash)*

10. We are meeting our friends at six-thirty. *(hyphen)*

Italics and quotation marks

Note: Although italics here are underlined to highlight that they have been added, never use both at the same time: use italics for printed material, and use underlining if you happen to be writing by hand.

1. Please look up the word *incoherent* in the dictionary.

2. I would like my steak served a la carte. *(correct as is; a la carte is common and needs no special treatment.)*

3. He has a new boat, which he named *Lucille*.

4. I flew on a Boeing 757 to Miami. *(correct as is)*

5. You have used *I* to begin your sentences too many times.

6. Please turn to Chapter 2, "The Order of Operations."

7. I was excited to see the movie *Star Wars* for the tenth time!

8. I always watch the television show *From Now to Then*, and my favorite episode is called "Going to the Future."

9. *Gone with the Wind* is a great book.

10. I just sent for tickets to the play *The Book of Mormon*.

11. I hired her because of her "I can do anything" attitude.

12. There was an article in *The New York Times* called "Children and Technology."

13. Judy said, "I think it is going to rain today."

14. Judy said that it will probably rain today. (*correct as is*)

15. The *Mona Lisa* is my favorite painting.

16. Please just answer yes or no! (*correct as is*)

17. It's raining cats and dogs this morning. (*correct as is*)

18. "'Yesterday' is one of my favorite Beatles songs," she said.

19. "I am running late," she said, "and I will probably miss the beginning of the movie."

20. The box was marked "fragile," so I put it in the closet right away.

Ellipses, apostrophes, and exclamation points

1. I need to buy bread, milk, and **apples** at the store.

2. "I think I forgot about . . ." she said as her voice trailed off, leaving her sentence unfinished.

3. Yikes! I left my wallet at the gym! (*You could also use just a comma after* yikes.)

4. I found **James's** book in my locker.

5. Do you know if **it's** supposed to rain today?

6. The **children's** clothes are getting wet out in the rain.

7. The dog left all its toys in the yard except the big green ball. (*correct as is*)

8. Do you know if these cookies are **theirs**?

Commas

1. It was a dark, stormy night in New York City.

2. The book that is lying on the table is overdue at the library. (*Take out commas.*)

3. I love reading mysteries; however, I don't really like thrillers.

4. In my opinion, that dress is to fancy for a birthday party.

5. I don't like to cook, and, by the way, I don't like to bake either.

6. After writing, new ideas popped into my head. (*Might be confusing without the comma.*)

7. In Rome do as the Romans do. (*correct as is*)

8. On the left side of the refrigerator sat the chocolate syrup I had been looking for. (*Correct as is—verb right after introductory phrases.*)

9. She was looking for you, so I hope she found you.

10. I went to the grocery store this morning and then came home and baked brownies. (*correct as is—not compound*)

11. I bought sugar, cocoa, baking powder, eggs, and cinnamon. (*optional comma after eggs*)

12. Raymond J. Fox, Sr. was my grandfather's name.

13. No, Rosa, I don't have any pizza left.

14. There are all kinds of books on the shelf, e.g., mysteries, romance, science fiction, and even some kid's books. (*The comma after fiction is optional.*)

15. I got up at 6 a.m., and I didn't go to bed until after midnight.

16. Don't wait up for me, because I will be home very late. (*Usually, there is no comma before because, but here it seems to need one. It is extra information. Compare it to this sentence in which I would not put a comma:* Don't wait up for me because you are worried! I will be fine.)

17. Since I am not going to the wedding, I will mail a gift to the couple.

18. The letter was dated August 1999. (*correct as is*)

19. The cat was very tiny, but very loud.

20. I am always right on time, never late.

Final test

1. I finished the project; should I send it to you? (*You could also use a period and capitalize should. Or, you could use a comma and add* so *after the comma.*)

2. My sister, along with her friends, is coming to visit.

3. He said, "I heard the song 'Forget You.'"

4. The new *Star Wars* movie didn't win the Oscar.

5. Bob was usually a quiet man; however, he screamed upon entering the room. (*You could also use a period after* man *and capitalize* however.)

6. To whom it may concern:

7. It is a cold, rainy day.

8. This book, which is written by William Golding, is my favorite.

9. The book that is on top of the table is next on my reading list. (*correct as is*)

10. I decided not to cook dinner and went to the movies instead. (*correct as is*)

11. I packed these three items for my hike: water, a jacket, and a knife. (*The comma before* and *is optional.*)

12. I was born on August 10, 1980, in Lincoln, Nebraska.

13. The only four ingredients in this recipe are sugar, vanilla, eggs, and flour. (*The comma before* and *is optional.*)

14. I did not do very well on the test, however, so I failed the course.

15. I think you should pack these clothes for the trip: jeans; shoes; black, brown, and white socks; and three shirts. (*The comma before* and white socks *is optional. The semicolon before* and *is necessary.*)

16. Yes, Elaine, the party is at my house.

17. My address is 1487 Markham Place, Boston, Massachusetts 01987; please send my mail there, not to my old address. (*You could use a period instead of the semicolon and capitalize* please.)

18. The word *collaborate* means to work together.

19. The self-confident student was on the debate team.

20. Please read the information on pages 60–85. (*en dash*)

21. My six-and-a-half-year-old cousin looks like my sister. (*hyphens*)

22. Jean Smith, M.D., has just started to work here.

23. Although this food tastes terrible**,** I will eat it anyway.

24. I failed the test because I didn't study. (*correct as is*)

25. **"**I am running late**,"** she said**,** **"**and I will probably miss the beginning of the movie**."**

26. I love his **"**can't fail**"** attitude.

27. I can't believe**,** since I didn't do anything wrong**,** that I got fired. (*You could also set off this interrupter with dashes or put parentheses around it.*)

28. Thomas**'s** book is on the counter.

29. Did I hear you say, **"**I am cleaning my room**"?**

30. That girl**—**she was in my class last year**—**is a cheerleader. (*You could use parentheses.*)

31. Whatever will be**,** will be.

32. Why I can't speak French after all those years of classes**,** I don't know.

33. "I don't know what I am going to do **...**" she said, her voice trailing off.

34. Who is going to sit at the cash register when you are on vacation**,** is my question. (*You could use a question mark instead of the comma.*)

35. I asked him if he could take care of the **dogs** when we are gone.

36. This summer I am visiting Idaho, Iowa, and Nebraska**;** and my sister will be visiting cousins in Boston. (*You could use a comma, but I think the semicolon makes the sentence clearer. You could also rewrite to avoid any possible confusion.*)

37. Charles Crumb (1874**–**1927) is buried here. (*en dash*)

38. Did you read the book *Training Cats: 101 Ways to Teach Your Cat Tricks?* *(Book title is in italics.)*

39. Hey! Watch out for the oncoming train! *(You could also use a comma after hey and a lowercase w in watch.)*

40. "I got all A's on my report card," the five-year-old student said.

Appendix C:
Glossary of Grammar Terms

Here is a list of some of the grammar terms that were used in this book.

Adjective   One of the eight parts of speech. An adjective describes a noun or another adjective and usually tells what kind or how many. *Examples: purple, pretty, seven*

Clause   A group of words that has a subject and a verb. *Example: That book, **which I read last night**, is a mystery.*

Compound adjective   Two or more words put together to describe a noun. *Example: self-defeating idea, high-back chair*

Compound sentence   A sentence with two or more independent clauses. *Example: I am tired, but I will go with you.*

Compound word   Two words that are put together to have one meaning. They can be written as separate words, hyphenated, or written as one word, depending on the word. *Example: e-mail, newspaper, fishing hole*

Conjunction   One of the eight parts of speech. Conjunctions are connecting words and often appear in compound sentences and series. *Examples: and, but, for, nor, or, so, yet*

Contraction   A shortened form of two words using an apostrophe in place of the missing letters. *Examples: I'm, you've, it's, she'll*

Declarative sentence   A statement. *Example: I am eating dinner.*

Dialog   Usually found in fiction writing, a conversation between two or more people, using quotation marks.

Direct quotation   The exact words that someone says. *Example: "Are we there yet?" he asked.*

Elliptical expression   A sentence or clause in which words are left out, but that is clearly understood. They are generally grammatically correct. *Example: Who is going? Not me.*

Fragment   A group of words that is intended to be a sentence, but instead is an incomplete thought. *Example: Because I said so*

Gerund   A verb form ending in *-ing* that is used as a noun rather than a verb. *Example: Reading is my favorite hobby.*

Imperative Sentence   A command. *Example: Open the door for me.*

Indirect question   A statement where a question is implied. *Example: She asked me if it is going to rain.*

Indirect quotation   Reference to what someone said, but not their exact words. *Example: She said that she didn't want any cookies.*

Infinitive   A verb preceded by the word *to. Example: to run*

Interjection   One of the eight parts of speech: a word that expresses emotion. *Example: ouch! wow! oh!*

Italics   *Tilted letters in print.* You cannot write in italics. To indicate italics in handwriting, use underlining.

Nonrestrictive clause or phrase   A group of words that is not necessary for the meaning of the sentence and is, therefore, set off with commas. *Example: That redheaded boy, who was in my class last year, is the valedictorian.*

Noun   One of the eight parts of speech: a person, place, thing, or idea. *Examples: car, dog, city, sofa, thought*

Participle A verb form, usually the past tense *(-ed)* or *-ing* form, that is used as an adjective. *Example: I drove past the **burning** building.*

Phrase A small group of related words that does not contain both a subject and a verb. *Examples: to the moon, hopping bunny, to be a painter*

Possessive pronoun The form of a pronoun that shows ownership. *Examples: my, mine, your, yours, his, hers, its, theirs, ours*

Preposition One of the eight parts of speech. A preposition is always the first word in a prepositional phrase. The phrase usually tells where or when. *Examples: in the box, after the party*

Pronoun One of the eight parts of speech. A pronoun takes the place of a noun. *Examples: she, this, who, someone, I*

Restrictive clause or phrase A group of words that are necessary for the meaning of the sentence and that are, therefore, not set off with commas. *Example: The girl **in the blue hat** is my cousin.*

Run-on sentence Two sentences with either no punctuation or a comma separating them. Either a period, colon, semicolon, or comma with a conjunction must be used to separate them. *Example: The flower is pink, it is very pretty.* This is incorrect.

Salutation A greeting, for example, the opening of a letter. *Example: Dear Dr. Smith:*

Sentence A group of words that contains a subject and a verb (an action and someone or something doing that action) and that is a complete thought. *Example: I throw the ball.*

Series comma The comma before the last item in a series, otherwise known as the Oxford comma. It is generally optional. I recommend using it. *Example: Lunch consisted of soup, a salad, and dessert.*

Text Writing hese words you are reading that follow each other and make sense.

Transition words   Words (or sometimes phrases) that connect one sentence or paragraph to the next, improving the flow and the sense of text. *Example: Next, you should add the sugar.*

Verb   One of the eight parts of speech. Every sentence needs at least one verb. Represents action or a state of being. *Examples: run, talk, cook, is, looks*

Appendix D:
Your Quick Guide to Commas

This quick guide to commas contains only the rules and the examples, without the explanations contained in the Comma section of the book.

1. Commas in compound sentences

A compound sentence is two (or could be more) complete sentences joined by a comma and a conjunction.

I am going to wash my car, and my roommate is going to mow the lawn.

Are you going to the mall, or are you going to work?

I would go shopping with you, but I don't have much money to spend.

If your compound sentence is really short, you can eliminate the comma.

She knits and she sews.

2. Commas in series

We use commas to separate the items in a series.

I need to buy apples, oranges, bananas, and strawberries for the fruit salad.

We are going to the mall, to the post office, to the pet store, and then to lunch.

I am going to work, my husband is going golfing, and the kids are going to camp.

3. Introductory elements

3.1 Introductory expressions and transition words

In my opinion, it is too cold to go swimming.

After all, the pool isn't heated.

Yes, I think I will go to the pool.

First, I think you should check the weather report.

3.2 Introductory prepositional phrases

In France we will stay with friends. (*In France* is short. No comma really needed.)

In France last summer, we stayed with friends.

3.3 Introductory participial and infinitive phrases

Hopping along the path, the rabbit stopped to munch a carrot.

Screaming, she ran from the house.

Throwing the ball, she shouted for me to catch it.

To be a doctor, you have to study for many years.

To go across the country, I had to change planes twice.

3.4 Multiple/combination introductory phrases

Running into the house with his dog, Jeremy asked for a cookie.

To be a teacher in a college, you need an advanced degree.

During my vacation in France with my mother, I met some relatives for the first time.

3.5 Introductory clauses

Since I started college, I have been very busy!

Whenever I think of my cousin, I think of all the fun we used to have.

After I eat dinner, I will watch TV with you.

Because I work early tomorrow, I need to get to bed early.

But there is usually no comma when you flip them around:

I have been very busy since I started college.

I think of all the fun we used to have whenever I think of my cousin.

I will watch TV with you after I eat dinner.

I need to get to bed early because I work early tomorrow.

4. Setting off interrupting material

I know, by the way, all about your secret

It is true, of course, that I will be elected the new president of the club.

The cake, chocolate with lemon icing, looks delicious.

Johann, my friend from school, was absent today.

Harry's mother, Joan, is wearing the same dress as I am.

When you need the interrupter for the meaning of the sentence, do not use commas.

Juan's brother Fernando was at the wedding. (Implies he has more than one brother.)

My neighbor across the street has a beautiful garden.

5. With *which* and *that*

Use *which* with nonrestrictive clauses, where the clause is added information, and set the clause off with commas. Use *that* with restrictive clauses and use no commas.

Who is usually used with people in both restrictive and nonrestrictive clauses. *That* is sometimes used, especially with tribes or groups of people.

The boy who is sitting in the front row is my brother. (restrictive; identifies which boy)

The boy I was talking about, who is a straight A student, is going to Harvard next year. (added information)

The street names in my town are named after the Native American tribe that settled there so many years ago. (Here we used *that*—and notice that this clause appears at the end of the sentence, rather than as an interrupter.)

6. In dialogue

Commas are sometimes used in dialogue and direct quotations in places where you might think there would be a period: the end of a sentence.

"Have another piece of pie," he said.

"I would have another piece of pie," she said, "but I am trying to lose weight."

She asked, "Does this pie have much sugar in it?"

He replied, "It must. It tastes awfully good."

She thought before answering. " I don't really know the answer to that."

7. Between two adjectives (sometimes)

Try putting *and* between the two adjectives. If it makes sense, use a comma.

She is wearing a bright blue dress.

Is that your new green bicycle?

That old, torn sofa is ready for the trash.

Please take that dirty, smelly sneaker out to the garage.

8. With *etc.*

Use a comma before *etc.* If *etc.* falls in the middle of the sentence, put commas both before and after it.

I like reading fiction, especially romance, chick lit, mysteries, etc.

Add the salt, sugar, flour, etc., before the wet ingredients.

9. With *i.e.* and *e.g.*

The initials *i.e.* mean "that is." The initials *e.g.* mean "for example"

I love music from the Classical era, e.g., Mozart.

The boy speaks only one language, i.e., English, his native language.

10. Direct address

Jose, please bring the newspaper in.

Please, Jose, bring the newspaper in.

Please bring in the newspaper, Jose.

Yes, Jose, you can come over to play.

11. Addresses

Please send me the information at my new address, which is 124 Sunny Street, Boston, MA 02216.

I live at 45 Elm Ave., Hunter, Idaho 67890.

I was born in San Francisco, California, in 1983.

We will be visiting my brother in Dallas, Texas, next month.

12. Dates

May 7, 2006

May 2006

My uncle has saved an article from the September 8, 1960, issue of *Time* magazine.

My aunt has saved the photo of a dress from the March 2000 issue of *Vogue*.

13. With numbers

Use a comma in numbers that contain four or more numerals.

5,000

7,000,000

Of the total of 575, 60 were children. (better to rewrite and avoid two consecutive numbers)

14. With *too*

I, too, would love to go to the concert.

Is Miranda coming too? (no comma necessary before *too*)

15. With academic degrees

Colleen Comma, Ph.D., will be speaking about punctuation.

Sandy Sailor, M.A., is the guest at the meeting.

16. With *Jr., Sr.,* and other titles

You do not need a comma after the title unless something right after the title is set off in commas—or the person prefers the title set off in commas.

Arnold Tyler, Sr. is my father.

Arnold Tyler, Sr., the director of the company, is my father.

17. Company names

ABC Widgets, Inc. (But if they write it without the comma, you should too.)

18. Salutations and closings of letters

Dear Mr. President: (formal letter)

Dear Joe,

Yours truly,

Sincerely,

19. With *however* and *therefore*

Therefore, I believe you should stick to the plan.

I am not sure the plan will work, however.

I know, however, that you will follow the rules.

I am not going; however, I know that you will take notes for me.

I am not going. However, I know that you will take notes for me.

Therefore works exactly the same way.

20. Afterthoughts

He is traveling to both England and France, I believe.

Joe isn't coming to the party, by the way.

That dress is too short, in my opinion.

He isn't coming with us after all. (You could put a comma after *us.*)

I knew he was lying of course. (You could put a comma after *lying.*)

21. Contrasting expressions

I like pizza, but not with anchovies.

He is my cousin, not my brother.

Pepperoni pizza, rather than vegetarian pizza, is my favorite.

Here today, gone tomorrow.

22. When *or* begins an explanation rather than a choice

Sometimes we use *or* in a sentence to introduce an explanation of something we just said. In that case, it is followed by a comma.

The drum major, or the leader of the marching band, is my brother.

Would you like to be the drum major or the bass drummer?
(In this sentence *or* is used in a choice, so there is no comma.)

23. To separate two of the same words in a sentence

As she explained it, it is a new type of printer.

If that is what the situation is, is she going to be able to handle it?

24. To clarify when a word is left out

The reason for the delay is, his mother is coming all the way from New York. (The reason for the delay is that his mother . . .)

Usually, if you leave out *that,* the sentence is still perfectly clear without a comma.

I know she doesn't like us.

Girls between four and six should line up here; girls between seven and ten, over there.

25. Unusual word order

Why he is choosing that college, I will never know.

That you will be late for dinner, I completely understand.

26. Emphasis

Occasionally commas can be used to indicate emphasis, but I wouldn't overdo it.

I agree, completely, with your conclusion.

She, herself, is planning her entire wedding.

27. Long question at the beginning of a sentence

You can use either a question mark or a comma if you begin a sentence with a long question.

How is he going to get all that done in time, is my question.

How is he going to get all that done in time? is my question.

28. Series of questions in a sentence

You can use either question marks or commas if you have a series of questions in a sentence.

Who is going to bake the cake? decorate the room? greet the guests?

Who is going to bake the cake, decorate the room, greet the guests? (Using the commas implies that one person is to do all these things.)

29. Clearing up confusion

A comma can be used in any sentence, when you cannot find any other rule, to clear up confusion.

After eating ants invaded our blanket.

After eating, ants invaded out blanket.

The dresses were pink with white polka dots and green with yellow polka dots.

The dresses were pink with white polka dots, and green with yellow polka dots.

30. Gray areas

One of the problems with knowing where to put commas is that sometimes you just have to decide for yourself.

Of course I will invite you. (Up to you whether to use a comma after *of course.*)

The little question marks in the sentences below indicate that you might (or might not) want to insert a comma.

Dogs and cats, horses and zebras, lions and tigers—even a unicorn—they are all here in these short stories ₂ full of magic and mystery.

"I want to be both a musician and the President when I grow up," said the little girl ₂ without a second thought.

No one had cleaned the garage in many years ₂ from the looks of it.

Index

a.m., 7
abbreviations, 6–8
   a.m., 7
   academic degrees, 7
   acronyms, 8
   decimals, 9
   measurements, 7
   p.m., 7
   people's titles, 6
   United States, 7
   with all caps, 6
academic degrees
   abbreviating, 7
   commas with, 82
acronyms, 8
addresses, writing out, 80–81
adjectives
   commas with, 78–79
   compound, 36
apostrophes, 59–62
   in possessives, 59–61
   plurals and, 61, 93
   possessive pronouns and, 60
   with contractions, 61
   with other punctuation, 62

because, comma use with, 74
Biblical references, colons and, 23
bibliographies, colons and, 22
book titles, colons and, 22
brackets, 31–32
   use in quotes, 31–32
   with parentheses, 31
business letters, 21

capitalization, colons and, 19, 23

clauses, introductory, 74
colon versus semicolon, 97
colons, 19–24
   Biblical references and, 23
   bibliographies and, 22
   book titles and, 22
   capitalization after, 19, 23
   compound sentence and, 15, 19
   greeting of business letter and, 21
   horizontal lists and, 19–20
   quotation marks and, 24, 54
   to express time, 22
   to introduce a quotation, 22
   vertical lists and, 20–21
   with ratios, 21
   works cited list and, 22
comma splice, 6
command, 5
commas, 67–91
   academic degrees and, 82
   addresses and, 80
   afterthoughts and, 84
   between two adjectives, 78–79
   clearing up confusion with, 87
   company names and, 83
   compound sentences and, 69
   contrasting expressions and, 84
   dates and, 81
   direct address and, 80
   essential/restrictive clauses and, 77–78
   for emphasis, 86
   gray areas and, 68, 87–88
   however and, 83–84
   in dialogue, 78
   in greeting of letter, 24

commas *(cont.)*
  introductory elements and, 71–74
  introductory phrases and, 72–73
  jr., sr., and other titles with, 82
  letter salutation and, 83
  nonessential/nonrestrictive clauses
    and, 77–78
  numbers and 81–82
  omitted words and, 85–86
  Oxford, 70, 71
  question at start of sentence and, 86
  quick guide to, 119–128
  separating two of the same word
    with, 85
  series and, 70,71
  series of questions in a sentence and,
    86–87
  setting off interrupting material with,
    75–77
  setting off words and, 95
  therefore and, 83–84
  transition words and, 72
  unusual word order and, 86
  versus parentheses, 27–28
  when not to use, 88–91
  with *e.g.,* 80
  with *etc.,* 79
  with *i.e.,* 80
  with *or,* 85
  with quotation marks, 54
  with *too,* 82
  which, who, and *that* and, 77
company names, commas in, 83
compound adjectives, and hyphens, 36
compound sentences
  conjunctions in 69
  semicolons in, 69
compound words, hyphens in, 35
confusion, comma and, 87
conjunction, 6, 70
  in compound sentence, 15
contractions, 61
contrasting expressions, comma in, 84

dashes, 39–43
  appropriate use of, 42
  em, 41–43
  en, 39–40
  interruptions in dialog, 42
  long, 41–43
  overuse of, 96
  placement in sentence, 41–42
  short, 39–40
  spacing of, 40, 42
  versus commas, 42
  versus hyphens, 35
  versus parentheses, 27–28, 42
dates, commas in, 81
decimals, 9
declarative sentence, 5
definitions, quotation marks with, 52
dialogue, 46
  commas and, 78
  dashes in, 42
  quotation marks in, 49–50
direct   questions, 6, 11, 12
direct address, commas and, 80
direct quotations, 49

e-mail greetings, 21
  commas in, 83
e.g., comma with, 80
ellipses, 57–58, 95
  definition of, 57
  omitted words and, 57
  trailing off and, 58
elliptical expressions, 9
elliptical questions, 11
em dash, 41–43
embedded questions, 11
emphasis
  commas and, 86
  italics for, 46
en dash, 39–40
  as minus sign, 39
  making on your computer, 39
  spacing around, 39
  with number ranges, 39

etc., comma with, 78
exclamation points, 5, 63–65
    general rules of, 64
    interjections and, 63
    questions and, 64
    quotation marks and, 54, 64

foreign expressions, and italics, 46
fractions, hyphens and, 36
fragment, sentence, 9

glossary of grammar terms, 115–118
gray areas, commas and, 87–88
greetings and closing of letters, commas
    with, 83

horizontal lists, 19–20
however
    commas with, 18, 83–84
    semicolon with, 17–18
hyphenated words, 35–36
hyphens, 35–37
    compound words with, 35
    in fractions, 36
    in spelled-out numbers. 37
    prefixes with, 35
    separating words with, 37
    spacing of, 37
    versus dashes, 35
    with expressions of time, 37

i.e., comma with, 80
imperative sentence, 5
indirect question, 6
indirect quotations, 50
initials, periods in, 9
interjections, exclamation points and, 63
interrupted dialogue, dash and, 95
interrupting elements, commas with,
    75–77
irony, quotation marks and, 50
italics, 45–47
    book titles and, 47
    for emphasis, 46

for words used as themselves, 45
foreign expressions and, 46
titles and, 47
to express thoughts, 46
versus quotation marks, 45–47

jargon, quotation marks with, 52
jr., comma with, 82

"labeled," quotation marks with, 52–53
letters
    commas in, 83
    in a list, 8
lists
    bullets in, 21
    horizontal, 19–20
    letters in, 8
    numbers in, 8, 21
    parentheses in, 28–29
    periods in, 21
    vertical, 20–21
long dash, 41–43

"marked," quotation marks with, 52–53
measurements, 7
minus sign, 39
multi-paragraph quotes, 96
multiple punctuation marks, using
    together, 96

numbers
    commas in, 82–83
    hyphens in, 37
    in a list, 8
    minus sign, 39
    parentheses with, 28–29
    ranges and en dash, 39

omitted words, comma and, 85
or, comma with, 85
outline, parentheses in, 28–29
Oxford comma, 70

p.m., 7

parentheses, 27–29
  brackets and, 31
  to set off additional information,
    27–28
  versus commas, 27–28
  versus dashes, 27–28
periods, 5–10
  command and, 5
  decimals and, 9
  declarative sentence and, 5
  elliptical expressions and, 9
  elliptical expressions and, 9
  in outlines and lists, 8
  indirect questions and, 6
  initials and, 10
  lists and, 21
  measurements and, 7
  quotation marks and, 54
  quotation marks and, 9
  to separate sentences, 5
phrases, introductory, commas and,
    72–73
plurals, apostrophes in, 61, 93
possessive pronouns, 60
possessives, 59–60
prefixes, hyphens and, 35
pronouns, possessive, 60
punctuation marks, unusual, 103–104

question within a sentence, 86
question marks, 11–14
  elliptical questions and, 11
  quotation marks and, 13, 54
questions
  direct, 6, 11, 12
  embedded, 11
  exclamation points and, 64
  indirect, 6
  series of in a sentence, 13
quiz
  answers to, 105–113
  commas, 90–91
  ellipses, apostrophes, and exclama-
    tion points, 65

final test, 99–101
hyphens and dashes, 43
italics and quotation marks, 55–56
parentheses and brackets, 33
periods and question marks, 14
semicolons and colons, 25
quotation marks, 49–55
  after "marked" or "labeled," 52
  around *yes* and *no*, 53
  book titles and, 47
  colons with, 24, 54
  commas with, 54
  dialogue and, 49-50
  direct quotations and, 49
  exclamation points with, 54, 64
  indirect quotations and, 50
  intentional spelling mistakes and, 51
  irony and, 50
  jargon and, 52
  periods and, 9
  periods with, 54
  question marks with, 13, 54
  sarcasm and, 50
  semicolons with, 18, 54
  single, 53, 97
  slang and, 50
  titles and, 47
  titles and, 51
  versus italics, 45–47
  with "abnormal" use or placement,
    51–52
  with definitions, 52
  with other punctuation, 54
  with well-known sayings, 53
  with words from another source, 50
quotations
  colon to introduce, 22
  comma to introduce, 22
  multiple paragraph, 96

ratios, 21
run-on sentence, 6, 70

sarcasm, quotation marks and, 50

sayings, quotation marks and, 53
semicolons, 6, 15–18
    sentence with series and, 16
    use with quotations, 18, 54
    versus colon, 97
    with *however*, 17
    with *therefore*, 17
sentence
    command, 5
    compound, 15, 69
    containing a series, 16
    declarative, 5
    exclamatory, 63
    fragment, 9
    imperative, 5
    run-on, 6, 70
    said in the tone of a question, 12
    separated with semicolons, 15
    unusual use of words in, 51–52
    using dashes in, 41
separating two sentences, 5
    with colon, 19
    with comma, 6
    with conjunction, 6
    with semicolon, 6
series
    comma in, 70, 93
    in compound sentence, 16
setting off words, comma and, 95
short dash, 39–40
single quotation marks, 53, 97
slang, quotation marks with, 51
sr., comma with, 82

that, comma with, 77–78
therefore
    commas with, 18, 83–84
    semicolon with, 17–18
thoughts versus dialogue, italics with, 46
time
    and colons, 22
    hyphens with, 37
titles
    italics with, 47
    quotation marks with, 47, 51
too, commas and, 82
trailing off at the end of a sentence, 58
transition words, and commas, 74

United States, abbreviated, 7

verb, 5
vertical lists, 20–21

which, comma with, 77–78
who, comma with, 77–78
word order, commas with unusual, 86
words
    from another source, and quotation
        marks, 50
    hyphenated, 35–36
    italics with, 45
    separating at end of line, 37

yes and *no*, quotation marks and, 53

About the Author

Arlene Miller, also known as The Grammar Diva, has written eleven grammar books, a self-publishing guide, and a novel. She also writes the weekly Grammar Diva Blog. When she isn't writing or blogging, she might be found copyediting someone else's book, teaching a grammar workshop, or giving an entertaining talk about words and language.

A former English teacher, technical writer, and newspaper reporter, Arlene has a B.A. in journalism, an M.A. in Humanities, and teaching and school administration credentials.

She wants you to know that she is quite a good tap dancer, plays a little piano, and loves coffee and music. But most important of all are her two children.

Originally from Boston, Arlene lives in Northern California with her small, but feisty, dog.

To find her blog and her books, please visit her website at www.big-words101.com (or www.TheGrammarDiva.com).

Contact and Ordering Information

The Grammar Diva's books are available from all online retailers in print and e-book format. They can also be ordered from any brick-and-mortar bookstore.

Contact Ingram or the publisher to order bulk quantities of any of The Grammar Diva's books for your school, company, or organization.

e-mail: info@bigwords101.com

website: www.bigwords101.com or www.thegrammardiva.com

Arlene Miller

THE GRAMMAR DIVA

23110706R00086

Made in the USA
San Bernardino, CA
21 January 2019